THE MARINE ETABLISSEMENT: NEW TERRAIN FOR CENTRAL AMSTERDAM

Published by:
Yale School of Architecture
180 York Street
New Haven, Connecticut 06511
www.architecture.yale.edu

Distributed by:
Actar D
355 Lexington Avenue, 8th Floor
New York, NY 10017
www.actar-d.com

This book was made possible through
the Edward P. Bass Distinguished
Visiting Architecture Fellowship fund of
the Yale School of Architecture. It is the
ninth in a series of publications of the
Bass Fellowship published through the
dean's office.

Editors:
Nina Rappaport, publications director
Owen Howlett ('13), assistant editor
David Delp, copy editor

Design: MGMT. design, Brooklyn, New York
Cover: Photograph by Mathew Suen

Library of Congress Control Number:
2016905658
ISBN 978-1-945150-07-4

THE MARINE ETABLISSEMENT: NEW TERRAIN FOR CENTRAL AMSTERDAM ISAÄC KALISVAART, ALEXANDER GARVIN, KEVIN D. GRAY, AND ANDREI HARWELL

YALE SCHOOL OF ARCHITECTURE THE EDWARD P. BASS DISTINGUISHED VISITING ARCHITECTURE FELLOWSHIP

Edited by Nina Rappaport
and Owen Howlett

09

Introduction

01

Fellowship Dedication 10

Introduction 14
Nina Rappaport and Owen Howlett

Overview

02

Studio Introduction 20
Alexander Garvin

Interview with Isaäc Kalisvaart 26

The Yale Studio

03

Studio Brief 42

Studio Projects 58
Jay Tsai, City Park
Hochung Kim, Artist Community
Jonas Barre, Konigin Beatrix Museum Tower
Owen Howlett, University City
Todd Christensen, Athletic Peninsula
Mathew Suen, De Nederland
Miron Nawratil, NieuwStedelijkCentrum
Jaeyoon Kim, Accelerator
Matthew Rauch, Emerald Harbor

The Work in Review

04

The Challenging Property Market and Student Response 122
Kevin D. Gray

Designers and Developers: Two Worlds Apart? 134
Erik Go and Hans-Hugo Smit

Next Steps for the Navy Yard

05

The Agile Transformation of a Navy Yard 146
Liesbeth Jansen and Maarten Pedroli

Closing Comments

06

Isaäc Kalisvaart 160

Biographies 168
Participants 173
Image Credits 176

A sidewalk scene near the Rijksmuseum in Amsterdam's Museumkwartier district

01

Edward P. Bass Distinguished Visiting Architecture Fellowship Dedication

In 2003, Edward P. Bass, a 1967 graduate of Yale College who studied at the Yale School of Architecture as a member of the class of 1972, endowed this fellowship to bring property developers to the school to lead advanced studios in collaboration with design faculty. Mr. Bass is an environmentalist who sponsored the Biosphere 2 development in Oracle, Arizona, in 1991, and a developer responsible for the ongoing revitalization of the downtown portion of Fort Worth, Texas, where his Sundance Square, which combines restoration with new construction, has transformed a moribund urban core into a vibrant regional center. In all his work, Mr. Bass has been guided by the conviction that architecture is a socially engaged art operating at the intersection of grand visions and everyday realities.

The Bass fellowship ensures that the school curriculum recognizes the role of the property developer as an integral part of the design process. The fellowship brings developers to Yale to work side by side with educators and architecture students in the studio, situating the discussion about architecture in the wider discourse of contemporary practice. The first Bass studio, led by Gerald Hines and Louis I. Kahn Visiting Professor Stefan Behnisch, in 2005, was documented in *Poetry, Property, and Place* (2006). The second Bass studio, in 2006, which teamed Stuart

Lipton with Saarinen Visiting Professor Sir Richard Rogers ('62), engineer Chris Wise, and architect Malcolm Smith ('97), was documented in *Future-Proofing* (2007). *The Human City* (2008) records the Yale studio collaboration of Roger Madelin and Bishop Visiting Professor Demetri Porphyrios. *Urban Integration: Bishopsgate Goods Yard,* which documents the studio led by Nick Johnson and the FAT architecture partnership, was published in 2009; Charles Atwood and architect David M. Schwarz's (M.Arch '74) studio work was published in *Learning in Las Vegas* in 2010. Katherine Farley of New York-based developers Tishman-Speyer and architect Deborah Berke, with Noah Biklen (M.Arch '02), led a studio that was featured, in 2011, in the book *Urban Intersection: São Paolo.* The studio of developer Vincent Lo of Hong Kong, with architects Paul Katz, Jamie Von Klemperer, and Forth Bagley (B.A. '02, M.Arch '05), was presented in the book *Rethinking Chongqing: Mixed-Use and Super-Dense* in 2014, and, in 2015, the studio of developer Douglas Durst and architect Bjarke Ingels was recorded in *Social Infrastructure: New York.* With this book, the ninth in the series, it is with pleasure that we present the research and design work of the studio led by Isaäc Kalisvaart, Kevin Gray, Alexander Garvin (B.A. '62, M.Arch /M.U.S '67), Andrei Harwell (M.Arch '06), Erik Go, and Hans-Hugo Smit.

Eastern view of
the Veemkade and
IJhaven docks

TE KOOP

Introduction to the Kalisvaart book
— Nina Rappaport and Owen Howlett

The Marine Etablissement: New Terrain for Central Amsterdam presents the design work of the M.Arch students of the ninth Yale Bass Distinguished Visiting Architecture Fellowship, taught by Isaäc Kalisvaart, CEO of MAB Development, with Alexander Garvin, Kevin D. Gray, and Andrei Harwell of the Yale faculty.

The Marine Etablissement, also called the Marineterrein, is Amsterdam's historic navy yard. Situated a stone's throw from Amsterdam's historic center, the 37-acre (15-hectare) site was a closed military installation for more than 350 years—a place all Amsterdammers could see but few could ever visit. Within the past few years, this situation has begun to change. The students' design projects and this book's related essays are a timely consideration of the opportunities and challenges presented by this rare and historic urban transformation.

The book begins with an introduction by Alexander Garvin, who provides a context for the studio's activities and design objectives. Next, an interview with Edward P. Bass Distinguished Visiting Architecture Fellow Isaäc Kalisvaart features Kalisvaart's important development work, both within Amsterdam and internationally, as the impetus for the studio and outlines larger aspirations for architecture and urban design within a development context. Following the studio brief and a summary of the studio participants, each student's design proposal is presented with master-plan drawings, diagrams, and renderings. The proposals for the Marine Etablissement display a wide range of approaches to design and representation, and the students were encouraged to focus on the strengths of their underlying ideas.

While the real-world development of the Marine Etablissement will be, ultimately, a long and complex political process with multiple agents and antagonists, the projects within this book illustrate the essential role of personal vision and imagination in the evolution of cities. Clearly, a diverse set of answers stems from a single question: what should be done with this extraordinary site?

In that regard, the third section of this book contains an analysis, written by Kevin D. Gray, lecturer in real estate at the Yale School of Management, that outlines the broad economic environment and financial feasibility of each design proposal—for a design studio, a rare exercise that informed the students' work along the way. Following Gray's piece, an essay by Kalisvaart's MAB colleagues Erik Go, head of Studio MAB, and Hans-Hugo Smit, senior market analyst at MAB, meditates on the nature of collaboration between designers and developers. Instrumental as co-instructors of the studio, Go and Smit share their observations about the students' response to the Marine Etablissement site relative to likely real-world outcomes.

Next, an essay by Liesbeth Jansen, project director of Marineterrein Amsterdam and former MAB employee, and Maarten Pedroli, of the Dutch planning consultancy Linkeroever, describes the current and ongoing plans that are being undertaken at the Marine Etablissement. As Jansen explains how her organization is working to open up the navy yard to the city, she defends the method of organic urban development behind the site's incremental transformation process. The book concludes with remarks from Isaäc Kalisvaart on the studio process.

The editors would like to recognize the work of the students who participated in the studio: Jonas Barre, Todd Christensen, Owen Howlett, Jaeyoon Kim, and Mathew Suen (M.Arch '13); and Hochung Kim, Miron Nawratil, Matthew Rauch, and Jay Tsai (M.Arch '14). We also extend our appreciation to our copy editor, David Delp, and graphic designers, Sarah Gephart and Olivia de Salve Villedieu, of MGMT. design, New York City, for their excellent work.

View of central Amsterdam from across the historic Oosterdok (Eastern Dock)

02

View of Prins Hendrikkade and the Zuiderkerk from a rooftop on Oosterdokseiland

Studio Introduction

— Alexander Garvin

Many architecture and planning problems are pursued in a vacuum, without regard to whether the resulting proposals might ever receive financing, public approvals, or enough interest to actually get built. The Yale School of Architecture established the Edward P. Bass Distinguished Visiting Architecture Fellowship as a way to introduce students to the complexities of these real-world issues. By bringing together designers with real estate developers, the program affords students the opportunity to gain insight into the demands of the client-architect relationship, the economic and legal realities of building, and the layered public context within which major projects must proceed.

Isaäc Kalisvaart, at the time the CEO of MAB Development, was designated the Bass Distinguished Visiting Architecture Fellow for spring 2013. He was assisted by MAB's Erik Go—head of Studio MAB, the firm's in-house architecture division—and Hans-Hugo Smit, senior market analyst at MAB, as well as Alexander Garvin (professor), Kevin Gray (critic), and Andrei Harwell (critic), all from the Yale School of Architecture. The project Kalisvaart selected for the studio is the best-located—and largest—undeveloped site remaining within any major city in Europe: the so-called Marine Etablissement, an underused, 37-acre, or 15-hectare, site located in the very heart of Amsterdam and owned by the Royal Dutch Navy.

The Marine Etablissement was presented to designers in the studio as part of the larger, 143-acre, or 58-hectare, Oosterdok, or Eastern Dock, development, which extends west to Amsterdam Central Station and southwest to the historic city center. This larger area boasts cultural institutions such as the Scheepvaartmuseum, the new Central Library, the Conservatory of Music, the Amsterdam Architecture Centre (ARCAM), and the National Science Museum (NEMO).

Nine graduate students spent four months devising individual proposals for the Marine Etablissement. The program opened with an introduction by the Kalisvaart team. Working as a group, the students collected information on the site and its surroundings, created site plans and three-dimensional models, and identified problems and opportunities for further analysis. At the end of three weeks, each student used the trove of research to devise an initial scheme that, they believed, reflected the vision and concerns of the developers and public agencies that would have the final say on the site's master plan. Then, after four weeks in the studio, the students traveled to Amsterdam for a week to see if their ideas made sense.

The Kalisvaart team created a remarkable sequence of events to introduce the students to Amsterdam as a whole and to the Marine Etablissement site in particular. A host of architects, planners, government officials, and representatives from ARCAM and the International New Town

Institute (INTI) met with the studio to discuss the site and the project and provide special insights into the proposals MAB was exploring. In response to the visit, each student adjusted his or her scheme to address the realities on the ground.

After eight weeks of intense work, each student presented very different initial site strategies to a panel of experts on large-scale urban redevelopment, including Carolien Schippers and Merijn Snoek (National Real Estate Agency), Maarten Kloos (ARCAM), and Ton Schaap and Paul Moons (City of Amsterdam). Although some students had to reconsider essential elements of their scheme following the review, all of them went on to develop a detailed master plan for the future of the Marine Etablissement. At the end of the four-month period, the results were presented to a jury that included Adib Cure, Frits van Dongen (the Dutch state architect), Jamie von Klemperer, Elizabeth Plater-Zyberk (M.Arch '74), Todd Reisz (B.A. '99 and M.Arch '03) and Lucy Wildrick.

Ideas proposed for the site included the creation of a new branch of the university; relocation of the opera house to a prominent location along the waterfront; establishment of a major conference center and hotel; and, in four separate schemes, creation of, respectively, a sports and recreation complex, an observation tower, an open lawn and performance shell, and an outdoor public swimming facility, which would become an ice-skating destination in the winter. The most radical proposal turned the entire site into a public park.

The students were asked to consider the highest and best uses for the site based on three criteria: physical and functional requirements, market demand, and community desire. The projects, however, went beyond the initial brief. For example, the most effective proposals paid special attention to the contextual demands of the areas surrounding the site, stressing access to the site in the form of streets, bridges, and tunnels in order to avoid vehicular congestion. Some proposals involved the judicious altering of nearby waterways or filling in sections of the harbor. Every development scheme, however, was proposed as a way to make Amsterdam an even more wonderful city.

All the participants of the studio worked in the hope that the ideas produced will help the people of Amsterdam to make good choices for the future of their city.

Concept rendering of MAB's now largely complete Oosterdokseiland development

Interview with Isaäc Kalisvaart

The following interview with Isaäc Kalisvaart is expanded from one published in the Yale School of Architecture's magazine, *Constructs,* Spring, 2013.

Nina Rappaport
How and why did you become a developer?

Isaäc Kalisvaart
As a Dutchman and son of a contractor, civil engineering in Delft was a logical choice of study. In my first job, I worked on the construction of large civil structures, most of the time in the Gulf region of the Middle East. However, over a period of several years, I realized that developing projects from the very start, rather than just building them, better suits my love for architecture, teamwork, and deal-making. So, I decided to get an MBA at INSEAD [Institute Europeen des Affaires, in Fontainebleau, France] and started in the development business, initially in the States and, much later, in Europe. I find being a developer to be fascinating because it is a very multidisciplinary profession. It requires an affinity for and understanding of finance and risks, design, engineering, process management, and it also requires the personal traits of good taste, optimism, and persistence. I am not pretending that I possess all these qualities, but I hope I have at least a few of them. And perhaps what is most important to me is that this business is about creating real places and spaces that can truly improve the quality of our cities. Over time, urban development has become my primary focus. Cities inspire me. I love their energy and believe they have a future because they interconnect people, goods, and information.

NR
You and your former company, MAB, have been developing large urban projects. When do you consider these projects successful?

IK
Good urban projects respect their surroundings and pay much attention to the quality of the public spaces. They are even more important for urban life than the architectural quality of the individual buildings and should entice people to wander around and stimulate temporary uses as markets and performances. Preferably, the design of

Amsterdam Central Library, Oosterdokseiland, Amsterdam: MAB Development

SkyLounge, Hilton Hotel, Oosterdokseiland, Amsterdam: MAB Development

the public realm is done in conjunction with the buildings and respects the historic urban structure of our older cities. Programmatically, I would argue that good urban development is about creating mixed-use places. Mixing public functions—libraries and theaters with residential units, state-of-the-art retail, restaurants, and workplaces—creates the 24/7 urban buzz that cities are all about. Mixing them in dense, accessible developments makes each component more feasible than it would be as a singular function. At the building level, architecture must respect its surroundings and allow for flexibility of future uses, which are probably the most important architectural qualities. Increasingly, we have transformed existing buildings to new uses, thereby answering the current demand for authenticity and sustainability. Like Jane Jacobs said, “New ideas need old buildings.”

NR

You just mentioned sustainability. How do you deal with the increasing calls for so-called sustainable development?

Oosterdokseiland, Amsterdam: MAB Development

De Rotterdam:
MAB Development

IK

First, cities are an important means to a more sustainable society. With current technological advances, cities offer growing opportunities for the recycling of organic and inorganic waste and the management of related flows, sometimes called “circular metabolism.” Within urban systems, mixed-use projects create additional opportunities for energy savings as different functions have complementary cooling and heating requirements—and, also, investments in shared underground cold and heat storage systems pay off. We have incorporated those storage systems in all our projects, such as the Oosterdokseiland in Amsterdam, a 250,000 square-meter, mixed-use development that sits next to the Central Station, where we even set up our own energy company to manage the system. This company can provide energy to its users for substantially less than the market price. The specific circumstances of a project can also create additional opportunities for energy efficiency. For example, we recently completed De Rotterdam, a 150,000 square-meter, mixed-use building that was designed by OMA. In that project, the building is cooled using the surrounding river water.

De Rotterdam: MAB Development

Even though CO_2-neutrality of buildings is quickly becoming the law of the land in Western society, a green building that generates lots of car traffic or leads to structural vacancy elsewhere is not really sustainable after all. However, high-density, mixed-use developments at transportation hubs, such as Central Station, that minimize travel distances, are.

De Rotterdam: MAB Development

Ultimately, architectural and urban quality might be even more important in terms of sustainability. People will always find new uses for buildings and places they love and not tear them down. I often use Amsterdam’s canal district as an example. The seventeenth-century buildings will never be destroyed and always find new uses over time.

De Rotterdam: MAB Development

NR

What are some of your favorite development projects and why?

IK

My first real experience with urban development was the transformation of a part of the forty-block area/site of former railroad tracks, called the River District, in Portland, Oregon. With a small group, we initially bought the highly polluted land that, over time, has been successfully transformed into a second urban heart for Portland. Although my involvement covered only the early phases, it has inspired me to focus on urban development ever since.

I will give you two examples of more recent projects, both located in Amsterdam. First, Oosterdokseiland, or ODE, which I mentioned before. This twelve-acre peninsula was occupied for over thirty years by the city's postal facilities and pretty much inaccessible. MAB initiated and won the

De Rotterdam: MAB Development

development competition with a master plan designed by Eric van Egeraat and our in-house team of architects, planners, and researchers. The plan restores the connection of downtown Amsterdam with its historic riverfront. Ten different architects worked on the design of the individual buildings and public spaces according to strict design guidelines that ensured both harmony and diversity. During a series of design studios, our international team of architects and urban planners created a cohesive ensemble of buildings and public spaces. The area now houses the Amsterdam Central Library and Conservatory of Music, large retail stores, Holland's second-largest hotel, cafés, restaurants, a public parking facility, and major corporation headquarters. These employers recognized that, in order to attract knowledge workers, they must be located in a truly urban environment. The good accessibility by both car and public transportation was another reason for picking ODE. The library and music conservatory have added to the attractiveness of this new part of town. They draw the millions of visitors that support the functions, such as the restaurants and cafés. The project also has some three hundred residential units, ranging from affordable housing to high-end penthouses, for all kinds of ethnic and socioeconomic backgrounds. With an FSI of 4.6, ODE has a higher density than any other mixed-use inner-city area in Holland.

Another project that I particularly like is the Westergasfabriek, which is where they used to extract gas from coke. Although the buildings were almost in ruins, their architectural appeal, enhanced by the contrasting green space in the middle of the city, was enormous. We considered the project as a laboratory for researching different forms of urban leisure and decided to put the preservation of the architectural and spatial qualities of the buildings first. We uncluttered the buildings to accommodate a variety of creative industries and various permanent cultural-leisure functions as well as provide flexible spaces for temporary events. Tenants and ideas were selected on the basis of maximum diversity and financial viability, so that the operations could sustain themselves in the long run. We put in state-of-the-art IT infrastructure to attract the media-and-communication sector as an anchor, next to the fashion industry, which was our second target sector. Next to a playhouse, dance studio, and a movie theater, you currently find there broadcasting studios, different restaurants and cafés, artists' studios, and a multitude of fashion entrepreneurs. The site accommodates major international events, such as the Amsterdam Fashion Week and the Holland Festival but also the annual Christmas market, neighborhood fairs, pop concerts, and the tattoo festival. Low and high culture meet here, making it a very urban place, indeed. The transformation has increased real estate values substantially in the surrounding neighborhood, which was largely populated by low- and middle-income households from a great variety of ethnic backgrounds.

NR

You have worked with many experienced architects who often have a specific direction in their work. How do you collaborate with them?

IK

We hire and sometimes fire architects. We do not select our architects primarily on their fame, but on the basis of their design vocabulary and track record in relation to our development vision for a project. Real estate development is teamwork with many stakeholders, including architects,

Westergasfabriek, Amsterdam: MAB Development

Westergasfabriek, Amsterdam: MAB Development

Westergasfabriek, Amsterdam: MAB Development

urban planners, city authorities, the general public, financiers, and so on. The developer, however, takes the majority of the risks and is paying the bills. I have always required our architects to be sensitive to our needs, as their client, and to show respect for the existing context and for budgets. More money does not necessarily create better buildings. Also, architects should not take design changes, required because of functional requirements or market developments, as an affront but, rather, as an opportunity to improve on their original designs. On the issue of collaboration, we often work with different architects for the various structures and public spaces in our mixed-use projects. However, some well-known architects are not very good at working together with colleagues. So, unfortunately, sometimes it is necessary to make changes in the design team and replace an architect, regardless of his or her stature. By the way, this has not happened with Rem.

NR

What do you see today as the major challenges and opportunities in developing urban projects?

IK

Large urban schemes often take up to ten years to develop. In one form or another, they are always public-private partnerships. Certainly, in Europe, you seldom encounter somebody such as Robert Moses, who single-handedly transformed Manhattan. Today, true leadership is often lacking in the public sector, and a shift has occurred from governing to governance, resulting in an overkill of regulations. Many local governments want full control over urban developments but push all the risks, including those related to planning and permitting, to the developer. Forging personal relationships and a common vision and having a clear division of tasks early on in the project's development have all increasingly become a prerequisite to any successful project.

With respect to the markets, if we look at the effect of the internet, the current demographic trends, and the focus on sustainability, growth is no longer the driver of property development. Particularly in Western regions, you see limited increases in population and consumer spending, mostly because of aging and little productivity gains. It is also difficult to get projects financed because of the increased regulation of the financial industry, especially after the recent banking crises. And institutional investors—our clients—are more and more risk-averse. Unlike before, they invest in projects only after a stable cash flow is reached. The difference in valuation between "good" and "bad" projects has increased dramatically, and many of our cities are coping with large vacancies and obsolete buildings, especially at suburban, mono-functional locations.

These structural trends are the new reality. Development is now about adding value, not square footage, and developers and architects have to do that by creating superior buildings and places. The shift from supply- to demand-driven development means a shift from quantity to quality. Development activity is concentrated on only the best urban locations. For me, developing our cities, including the redevelopment of existing buildings, is the superior response to dealing with the growing scarcity of natural resources as well as meeting people's needs.

The Bass studio is meant to build an in-depth understanding of the role of design and the designer in the practice of real estate development. Together with my MAB colleagues Erik Go and Hans-Hugo Smit, I formulated a number of additional requirements for the studio's topic, such as creating a truly urban and real-life development opportunity, an inspiring location, and a contextual project, rather than a tabula rasa. We also wanted the students' work to be meaningful to the public discourse.

As an object of study for the Bass studio, the navy yard met these requirements, as it is one of the most important and largest undeveloped sites remaining within any major city in Western Europe. It is an underused, 15-hectare site, located in the very heart of Amsterdam. Its history is part of the DNA of every Dutchman, and it is not just a theoretical development project: After more than 360 years of naval history, the national government has agreed to hand it over to the city. Plans are in progress for its future development, and those plans are hotly debated. During a meeting with Dean

Westergasfabriek, Amsterdam: MAB Development

Westergasfabriek, Amsterdam: MAB Development

Robert Stern and professors Alexander Garvin, Kevin Gray, and Andrei Harwell, we proposed this site, and they were immediately enthusiastic. We agreed that the assignment would include an overall development strategy and master plan for the site as well as a specific building project within the site's boundaries. The plans also had to add something unique to the urban fabric of Amsterdam. The studio grappled with important disciplines, including programming and supply-and-demand market analysis, planning and zoning, financial feasibility, budgets and funding, and risk-mitigating strategies, such as phasing, co-ownership, and programmatic flexibility.

As originally planned, the student's work was exhibited at ARCAM, the Architecture Center of Amsterdam, and was the focal point of discussions among various stakeholders and the general public. An important topic was whether the initial approach to the site's transformation should be the implementation of an ambitious public program, as suggested by most students, or a gradual, organic development process.

03

View from a roof terrace on Oosterdokseiland toward central Amsterdam

Studio Brief

In this studio, students were asked to consider and understand the relationship between the commercial development process, site master-planning, and individual building projects while looking at one of the most important—and largest—remaining undeveloped sites within any major city in Europe. The Marine Etablissement, an underused, 37-acre (15-hectare) site located in the very heart of Amsterdam, will be redeveloped in the coming years, and its planning will engender significant public debate within the Netherlands. Through their work, students in the Bass studio had the opportunity to add to that debate with their ideas on program, urban framework, and architecture.

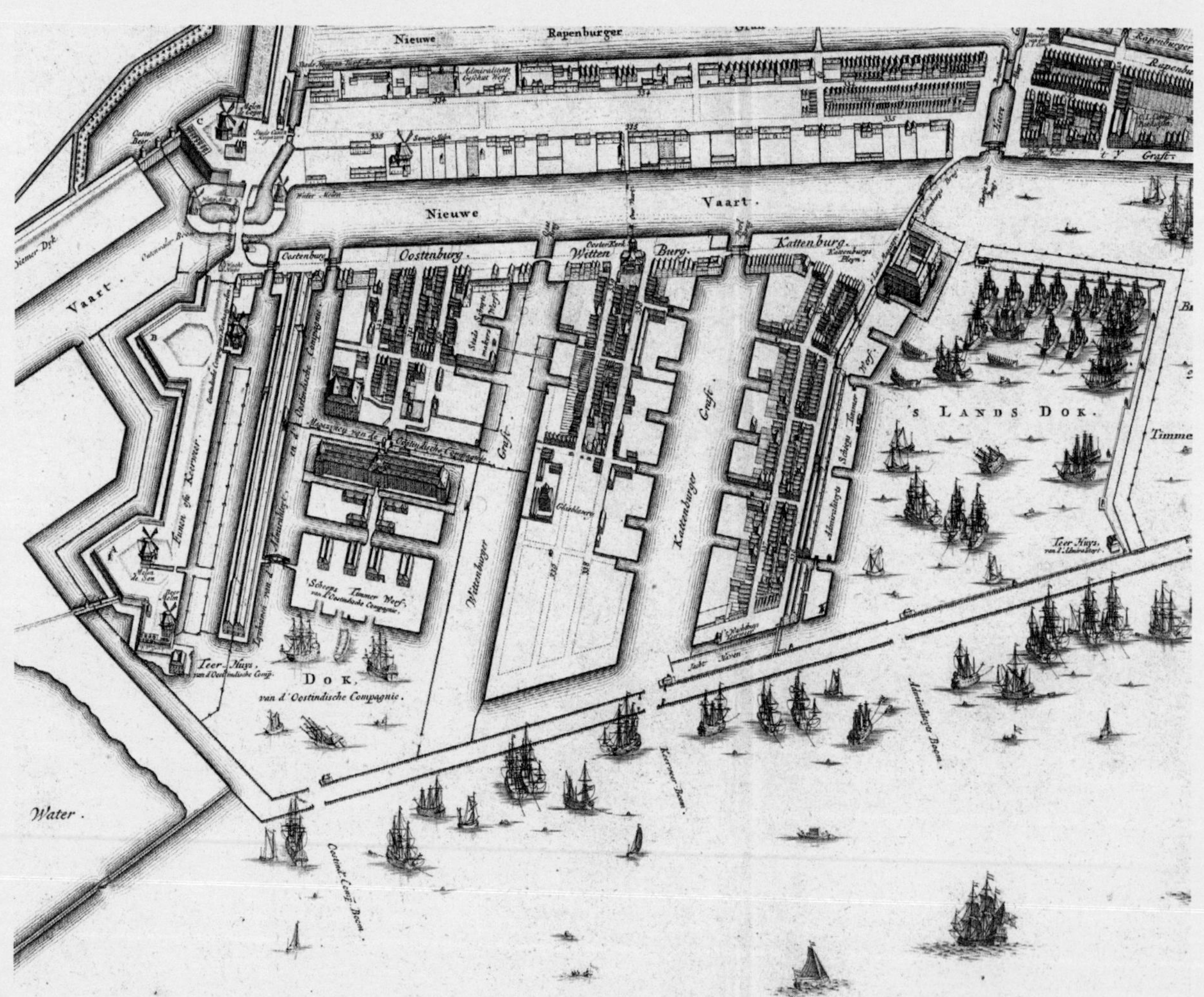

A 1792 engraving by Gerrit de Broen of the Oostelijke Eilanden section of Amsterdam, with the Marine Etablissement at right

A Storied Past, an Open Future

View of the Marine Etablissement and the Lands Zeemagazijn (Arsenal building) in a 1726 engraving by J. Mulder

The Marine Etablissement, or Naval Installation, site has a storied past that is part of the golden age of Dutch maritime history. Similar to the Arsenal in Venice, this site was for centuries the place for boat construction and the launching of the Dutch fleet, an important factor in Dutch global trade and suggestive of the country's influence around the world. The site has been part of the Dutch Admiralty since 1654. Significantly altered over the years and occupied by only a few buildings of historic importance, the Royal Dutch Navy, the City of Amsterdam, and other stakeholders will be coordinating plans to develop this important site in the near future.

Students had the unusual opportunity to consider this important site in the context of current market forces and participate, in real time, in the development process from its inception, change to collaborating with real developer-clients, other stakeholders, and government and military officials.

The Assignment

Although the students were architecture students—and not real estate developers—the aim of this studio was to consider design and the role of the designer from the perspective of the developer. Students were asked, therefore, to prepare an overall Development Strategy and Master Plan for the Marine Etablissement site and to design a specific Building Project within the site. In order to achieve their respective visions, the students had to grapple with numerous disciplines, including, among others, programming and supply-demand market analysis, planning and zoning, financial feasibility, budgets and funding, and development risk-mitigating strategies, such as phasing, co-ownership, and programmatic flexibility.

The Zeemagazijn—the Arsenal Building of the Dutch Admiralty, ca. 1656—with the Marine Etablissement site in background at left

Site Description

The Marine Etablissement is a centrally located area in Amsterdam of approximately 37 acres (15 hectares) and currently owned by the Royal Dutch Navy. Located within the eastern harbor area, it is bordered by the Oosterdok (Eastern Dock) to the west, the Oostelijke Eilanden and Kadijken to the southeast and the Dijksgracht-railway tracks-Oostelijke Handelskade to the north. It is located on an island and accessed from Kattenburgerstraat.

The Marine Etablissement is understood as being a potential part of the larger, 58-hectare Oosterdok redevelopment, which includes the former docks and extends to the Amsterdam Central Station to the west and the historic city center to the southwest. Within this area sit important cultural institutions, such as the Scheepvaartmuseum, the new Central Library and the Conservatory of Music (both developed by MAB), the Amsterdam Architecture Center, and the National Science Museum (NEMO). Part of the Eastern Dock is a large, mixed-use scheme, called ODE, by MAB Development. The Marine Etablissement site offers a unique opportunity to study a major undeveloped site in a major European city. In Amsterdam, it is the only large area close to the city center that is still to be developed. It is not master-planned, nor has it been a part of any extensive study, due to its longtime ownership by the Dutch Royal Navy and security restrictions. It is expected to be on the market in the future as part of a privatization effort. Its future use is high on the agenda of both the City of Amsterdam and the national government. It has a rich history.

The combination of the Oosterdok and the Marine Etablissement allows for planning and study in the broader context of land, water, infrastructure, and programming in both contemporary and historic surroundings.

Pre-Studio Development Status

The Royal Dutch Navy, the owner, announced plans for the sale of the Marine Etablissement site in 2010. In October 2011, an information evening was organized to discuss the future of the Marine Etablissement and its importance for the city. Public and government interest was understandably high.

A special task force, which included both city and state officials, was set up to define the ambition for the site. Suggesting high hopes, the general sentiment was that this redevelopment should not produce just another residential area. Indeed, the site seemed ripe for a special combination of urban

Aerial photograph of central Amsterdam with the Marine Etablissement site at top right

programming. Local parties of interest were very enthusiastic about the Yale studio, and Yale was offered the rare possibility to access this Royal Dutch Navy site.

As part of its development of the Oosterdok, MAB prepared preliminary maps that showed the links between the island and the city, but which apply equally to the whole Oosterdok, including the Marine Etablissement site.

Studio Participants

The Bass studio project offered students valuable interaction with an array of participants from all levels of Dutch society, business, and government:

Municipality of Amsterdam (Gemeente Amsterdam)

The municipality of Amsterdam and the national government are the prime stakeholders in the Marine Etablissement and its future development. While they were in an early phase of defining an optimal approach to the development of the site, MAB asked the municipality to participate in different ways in the Yale studio. The officials provided background information on the location, its surroundings, and the planning and political processes that will lead its development. In return, they, hopefully, benefited from the architecture students' ideas and the exchanges with Yale faculty in finding the right approach to the site's development. The city was represented by its project director for the IJ Riverbanks, urban planners, and the alderman, responsible for urban development.

View east from Oosterdokseiland toward the Marine Etablissement site, with Piet Heinkade at background left

MAB Development

MAB and the Yale students worked together with the municipality and other stakeholders on a study that was beneficial for mutual understanding and the framing of conceptual ideas, all of which may be helpful in future developments. The results of the studio provided insights into new development

View north from Marine Etablissement Site: houseboats and new development along Piet Heinkade beyond

strategies—public-private partnerships, tax exemption zones, among others—and, aims to, advanced public awareness and dialogue.

ARCAM (Amsterdam Architecture Centre)

ARCAM and its director, Maarten Kloos, an architectural historian, was an important source of information on architecture and planning in the Netherlands and Amsterdam as well as the history of the surroundings of the studio site. Kloos is a prolific thought leader on urban development in Amsterdam and was a valuable participant in the workshops with the students. ARCAM is a neighbor and a potential future user of the Marine Etablissement site and provided the Yale students with studio facilities during their time in Amsterdam.

View of the Marine Etablissement site from across the Oosterdok

The studio visits ARCAM's exhibition of past design proposals for the Marine Etablissement site

Learning Objectives

The primary learning objective of the Bass studio was to gain an in-depth understanding of the role of design and the designer in the practice of real estate development as well as the mutual dependency between, on the one hand, the development process and developer and, on the other hand, the design and designer.

Students gained specific knowledge of how MAB, as a real estate developer, looks at the world, the business opportunities it offers, and its perspective on the role of design and the designer. The students also gained insight into how MAB works as a real estate developer (strategy, tactics, operations), from raw site to finished product, and what that means for the role of design and the designer. Together, the studio participants mastered a working knowledge of the Dutch development context (urban planning systems, public-private partnerships) and market trends (residential, office, retail, and leisure), with a focus on those aspects that are most relevant for, and transferable to, other markets. The students had to demonstrate an ability to design a plan for redevelopment that would be feasible from a spatial, market, political, and financial perspective and, as an additional objective, the ability to draw parallels and recognize differences between Dutch ("Rhineland") and U.S. ("Anglo-Saxon") approaches to complex processes such as development, with new strategies drawn from U.S. practices for the benefit of MAB, the City of Amsterdam, and the Dutch real estate community.

Work Product

Students in the Bass studio formulated a Development Strategy, a Master Plan, and a Building Project within the Marine Etablissement site. They also prepared, with the assistance of the faculty, supporting market and financial data typical of what is required by a real estate developer to determine both the investment decision (is there a market?) and the finance decision (is the return on cost attractive?).

The work product included a vision for the site that was developed through physical planning, analysis, and design; however, this vision concerned more than just the physical, including the technical, aspects of the site and its surroundings. Other relevant parameters—such as the market, financial feasibility, and political viability (public and political consent)—influenced the design process and were critically considered and represented.

Late Modernist-era administrative buildings at the Marine Etablissement site

Questions that were addressed in the formulation of the work product included:

Users

—What are the strengths and weaknesses of the program (housing, shopping, office, public functions) from a user point of view?

—What would be an ideal program for the site from a market supply-and-demand point of view?

—How "marketable" is a given program?

—What program elements would best meet the individual customer's needs?

Financial Parameters

—How will the design affect the sources and uses of capital for development?

—How will the design affect the potential funding structure?

—How will the design affect operating costs, or expenditures?

—What are the major sources of potential operating income, and how will the design affect the total operating income?

—What is the traditional Dutch way of approaching such developments (public-private partnerships, residual land price, and so on)?

—What U.S. practices (tax-exempt government bonds, low-income-housing tax credits, TIFs, BIDs, and so on) could be implementable?

Community: Public and Political Consent

—How can possible controversies be evaluated from a public or political point of view?

—What method of public involvement should be implemented in the planning process? What would be an ideal program for the site from a community point of view, and what are its problems, drawbacks, and potential deal-breakers?

—Which potentially profitable and desirable program elements would be politically "controversial"?

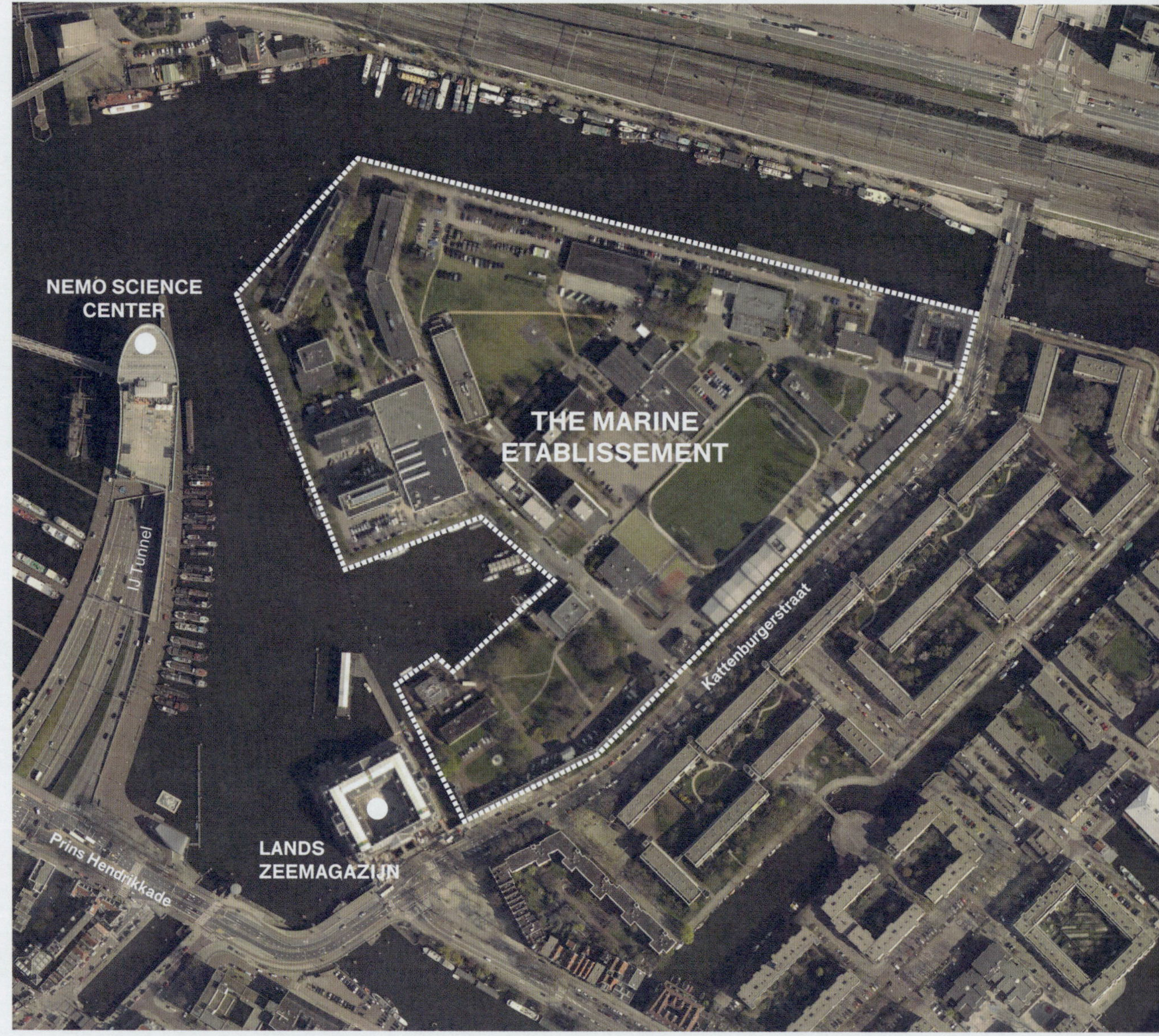

Aerial photograph showing the 15-hectare Marine Etablissement site

The Development Strategy and Master Plan were presented at the studio midterm, and the final projects, including the students' Building Project and supporting data, were presented at the final studio review.

View across the Oosterdok harbor toward the NEMO center

Historic buildings along the Geldersekade canal in central Amsterdam

Studio Projects

Jay Tsai, City Park

Situated in a sensitive yet neglected site, the new proposal for the Marine Etablissement requires an intelligent response to the political players, the urban fabric, and the community. This project creates an iconic park for the City of Amsterdam. The idea behind the proposal is to give the site back to the city and people of Amsterdam, enriching the local area.

To tease out a solution, research started with an analysis of the city's existing public amenities. The Marine Etablissement is surrounded by low-lying residential neighborhoods on the east and south sides, offices on the northeast side, and cultural and recreational amenities on the west side. Taking this into consideration, research continued on the architectural and spatial possibilities that could cater to these areas. Stepping out of the train station, one cannot help but notice how the Marine Etablissement site is architecturally disconnected from the area surrounding it. Unsurprisingly, most people head toward the UNESCO designated heritage site of old Amsterdam, where there are plenty of shops, restaurants, museums, and other attractions. However, one hundred meters

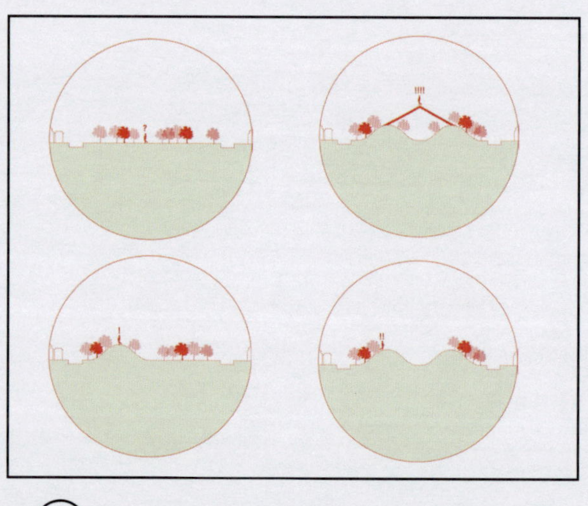

01

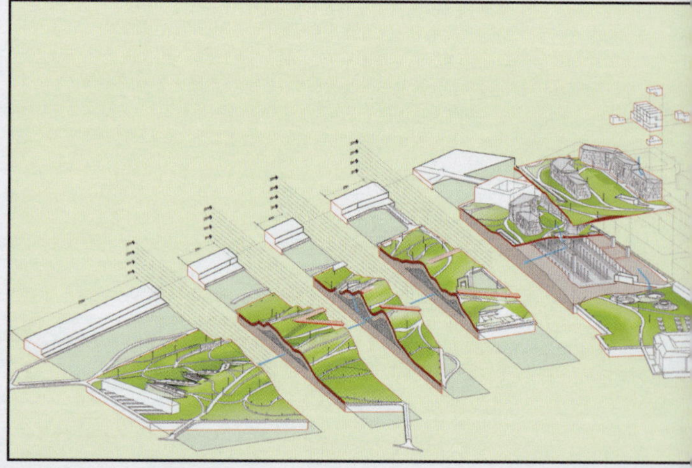

02

01
Section diagrams showing the integration of the hill and pedestrian bridge

02
Exploded axonometric diagram of the site showing topographic variation and green area

03
Aerial plan of the site showing walkways, green areas, and pedestrian connections to NEMO and Oosterdock Island

03

04

04
An iconic image for the new site featuring the bridge

05
View back toward central Amsterdam from the top of the bridge

06 (overleaf)
The new park as seen from the adjacent NEMO, with recreational open space in foreground

to the west of the site is a new potential anchor point, the Openbare Bibliotheek, the new public library. The area adjacent to this anchor point lacks open space, as does central Amsterdam in general. As public parks are used daily for sightseeing and as a lunch spot for workers, a place to play for children, and a scenic route for bicyclists, this public feature could reconnect a historically disconnected area and jump the many political hurdles that are needed to redevelop the Marine Etablissement site.

Given the size of the site, a park appeared to be an ideal spatial solution. To activate the park and get people there, the proposal offers something that is absent in Amsterdam: a hill with an iconic pedestrian bridge. Here, a hill produces an undulating sequence of spaces, which open up vistas toward the City of Amsterdam and create "ah-ha" moments in the park. The focal point of the design is the iconic bridge, which is a symbol for the surrounding neighborhood and attracts visitors from a distance.

(05)

06

Hochung Kim, Artist Community

This proposal offers an Artist Community to enhance the quality and attractiveness of living in this urban environment. The design was partly inspired by the canals of Venice Beach, in Los Angeles, and the dense residential artist neighborhoods in Southeast Asia. Numerous studies were made to investigate how a mix of art, art institutions, artist workshops, and housing could work. Initial solutions that involved large-scale art institutions concentrated along Kattenburgerstraat or interspersed throughout the entire site were abandoned for a much smaller-scale approach. A seemingly arbitrary grid is projected over the site, allowing for the creation of public, semi-public, and private spaces. The unfolding of the art theme follows the same gradient: from civic art that is accessible to all to the private workshop of the artist. The proposal includes a typological study of housing. Further, density and the ratio between infrastructure, public space, and private land have been studied in order to clarify and quantify the development potential of the Marine Etablissement.

Historically, the site has been isolated because of the military's security concerns. One of the design's main objectives is to re-purpose this isolation by creating the Artist Community, a semipublic development in which the residents will have access

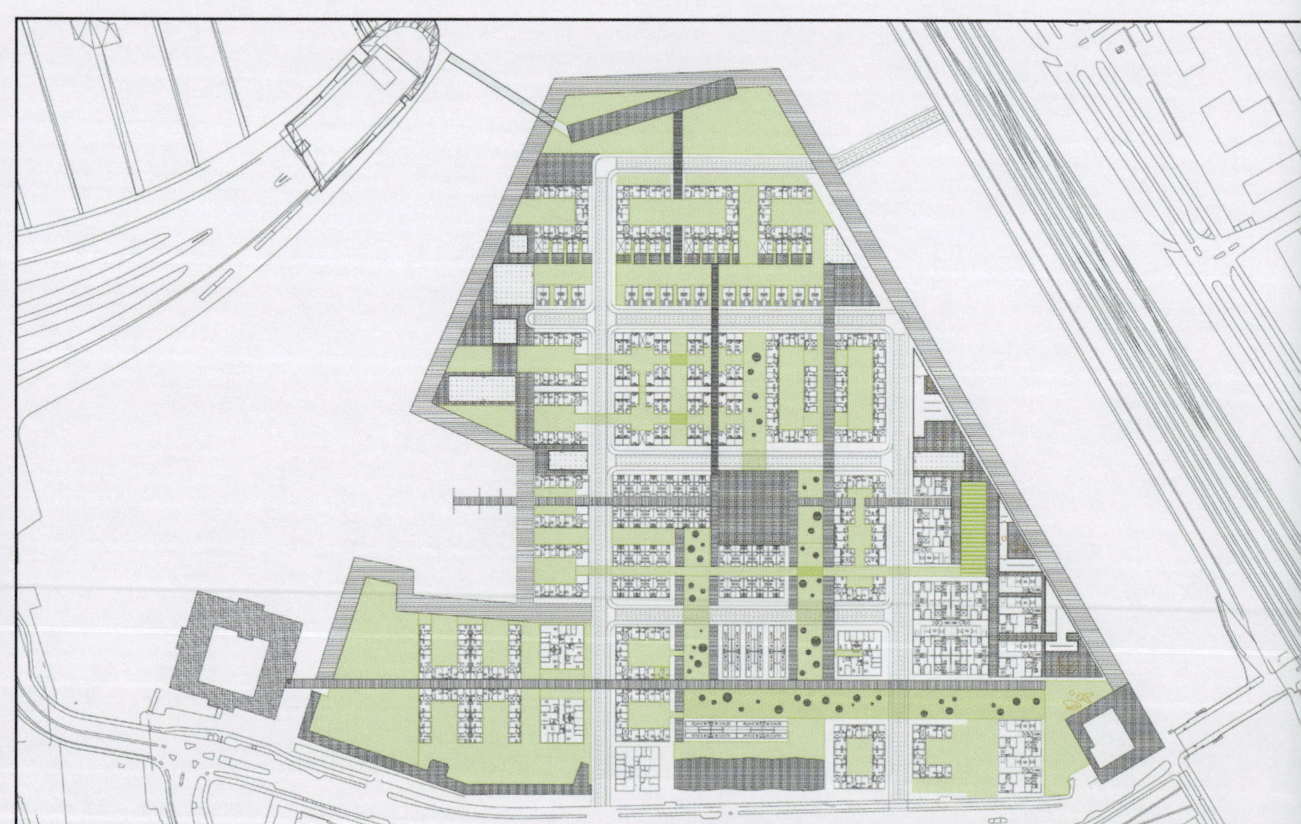

01

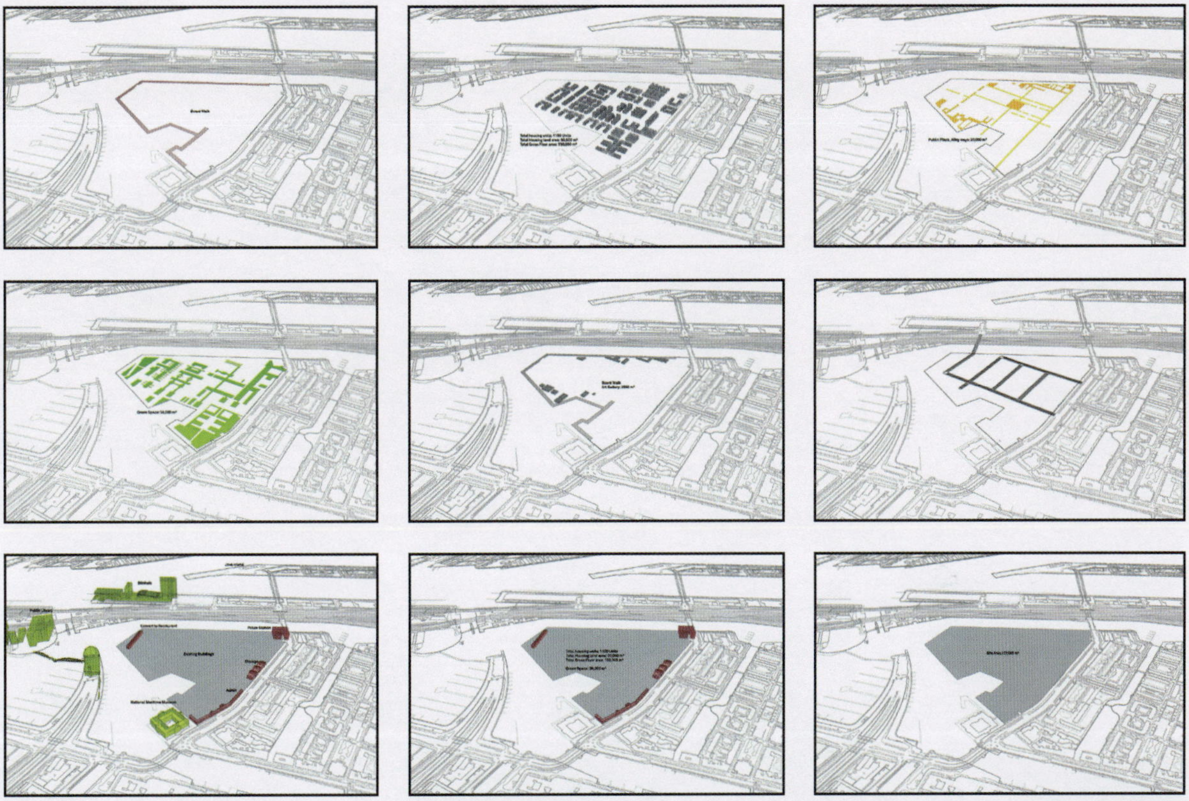

(02)

(03)

01
Site plan for the Artist Community showing a mix of housing typologies at a range of densities

02
A series of diagrams showing site improvements, preserved buildings, and the existing cultural context

03
Perspective view showing open space and a block of artist residences

04

to private galleries for various events. Sculpture gardens sit between the apartments to activate social interactions within the community. During the research phase, various housing typologies were introduced to gain insight into current Amsterdam housing units, and new typologies were suggested to create small, intimate green spaces in between the buildings. The site, which will be developed mostly through private companies, must maintain the continuity of the community's architectural language but also introduce new and different spaces. The design emphasizes new ways of looking at housing units in relation to the public roads. In short, the design creates community while maintaining the site's isolation.

05

04 (previous)
Aerial perspective of site, looking west, with central Amsterdam in the background. The disposition of housing types shows the mix of smaller, more intimate green spaces and sculpture gardens

05
Plan diagrams showing housing typology precedents and four different configurations of open space and residential units

Jonas Barre, Konigin Beatrix

Museum Tower

Attracting millions of people from around the world, Amsterdam is one of the prime tourist hubs in Europe. However, while New York City has the Empire State Building, Paris has the Eiffel Tower, London has the Eye, and Singapore has the Flyer, Amsterdam's skyline lacks a true landmark that defines the city's identity.

Famous landmarks are tourist destinations in and of themselves. Further, they are a source of revenue; for example, yearly ticket sales from the visitors to the Empire State Building viewing platform dwarf the actual rental income from the offices in the building. The Marine Etablissement site is the perfect location in Amsterdam for a proposed Museum Tower, outside the historic center while its viewing platform allows visitors to appreciate the concentric layers of canals radiating outward.

The capitalized cash flow from the proposed viewing tower would be enough to pay for the development of significant public amenities at the site. The Museum Tower could finance a building for the

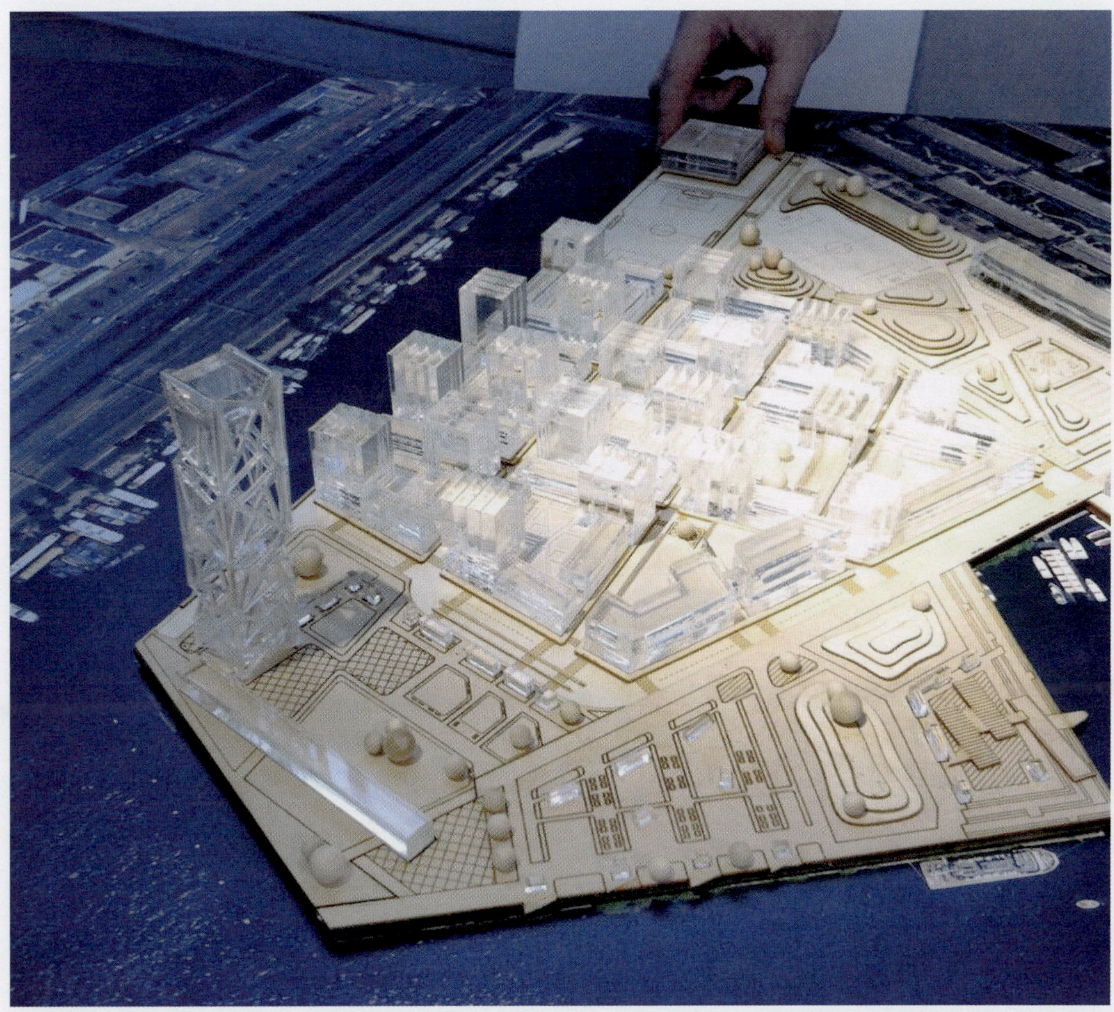

01

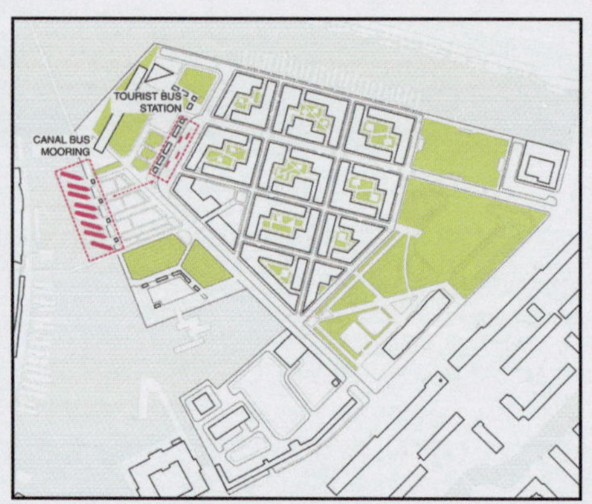

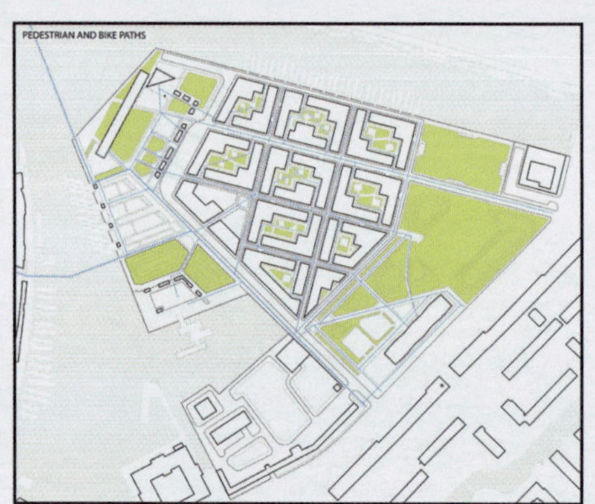

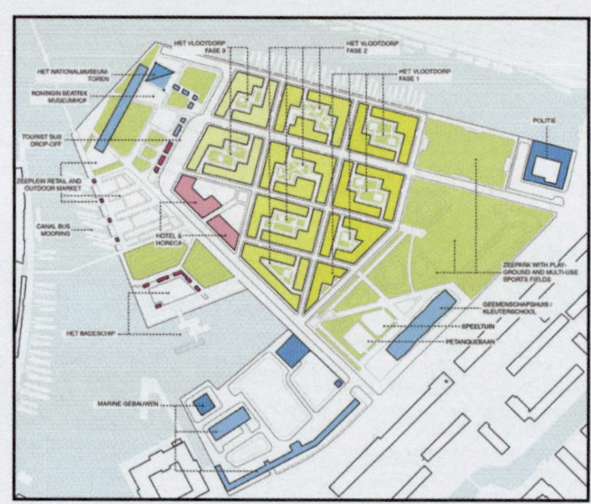

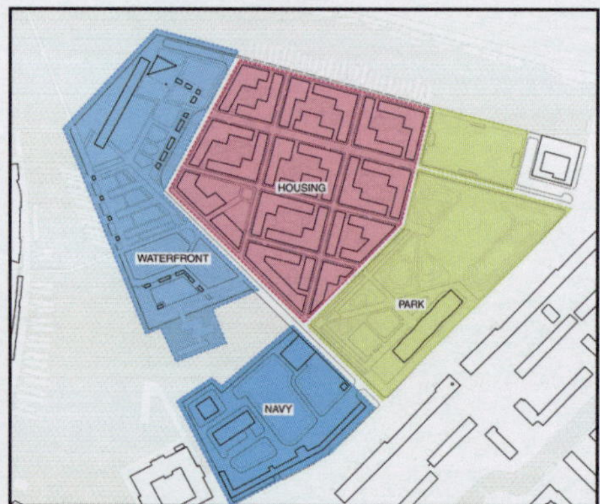

01 (previous)
Model photograph showing the Museum Tower and residential blocks

02
Site plan diagrams showing uses of key buildings, major circulation, and site zoning

03
View of observation tower from the waterfront public space

04
Site section from an eastern perspective, with Museumhof and tower at left

national museum, extensive parkland with much-needed public football fields, an outdoor pool-barge, or an outdoor market place. Most important, the Museum Tower could enable a significant investment in affordable—that is, under 100,000 euros—owner-occupied micro-scale apartments for young professional university graduates—something in short supply in the current central Amsterdam residential stock.

The Dutch navy will preserve some of the site for ceremonial and administrative uses—the historic walls and, for functions and events, the admiral's house will remain—continuing the navy's century-long presence.

Museum Tower transportation—via bus, train, or canal boat—in and out of the area will be separated from the residential road network, facilitating visitor traffic.

03

04

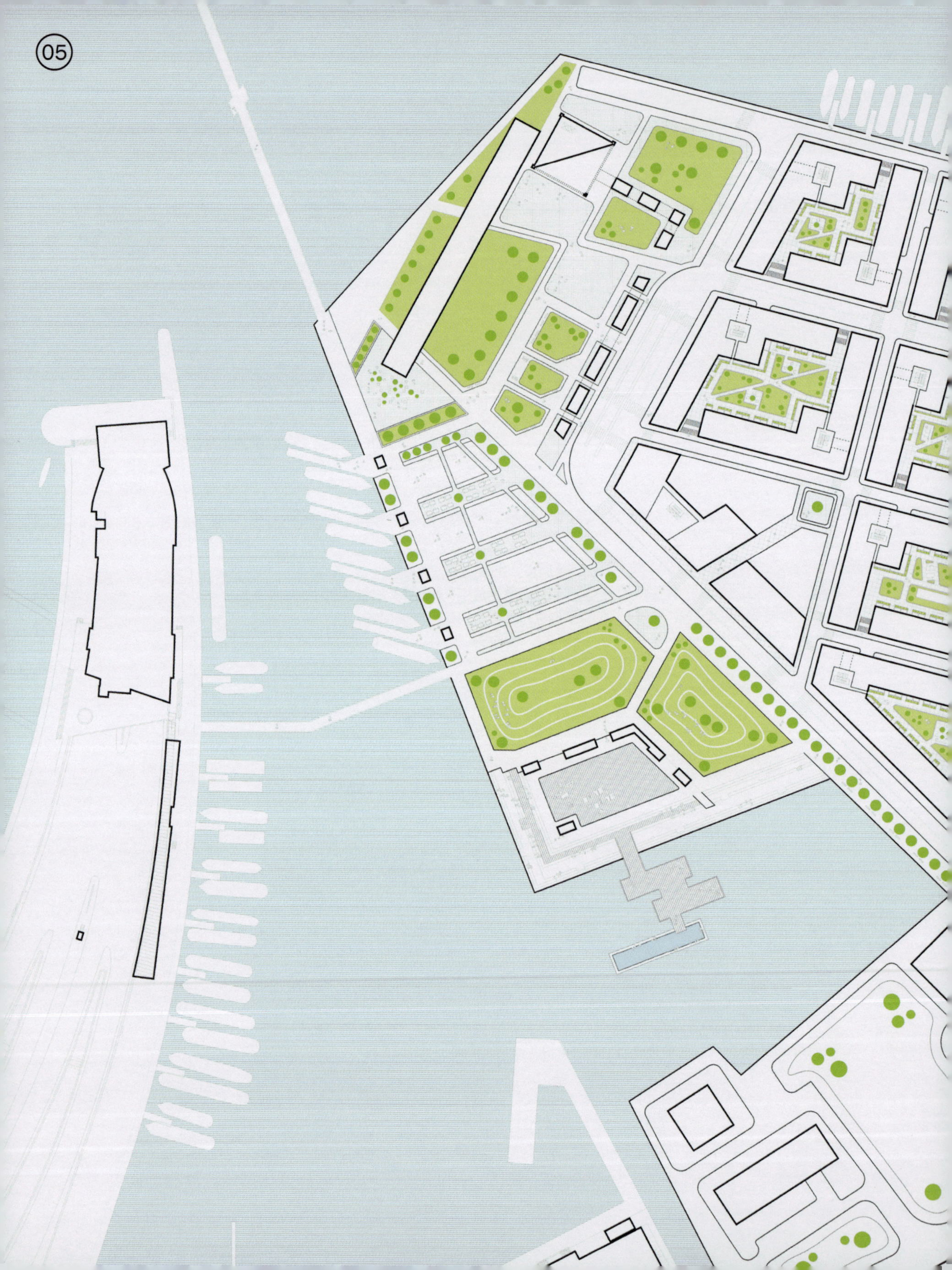
05

06

05 (previous)
Site plan of the Museumhof showing the tower at the top left and the residential blocks in the middle

06
Close-up view of observation tower and the National Museum arrival area

Owen Howlett, University City

University City is a proposal to transform the Marine Etablissement site into a new urban district with a new, world-class university at its core. Comprising twelve buildings and more than 140,000 square meters, the proposed university for applied sciences and technology is surrounded by 115,000 square meters of housing for city residents, students and researchers, new shops, and cafés, as well as a series of public squares and parks, to provide much-needed outdoor recreation and leisure space for residents of the entire city. The founding of a large-scale university campus in the center of Amsterdam would be an unprecedented investment in the city's future and a new use for the historic navy yard, befitting its national significance and five-hundred-year history.

Three highly distinct public spaces define the proposal: the Marine Basin (a new public beach and promenade), the Etablissement Park (University City's connection to Amsterdam's Central Harbor, the Eastern Docks, and the NEMO science center), and the Academic Quarter (a public square lined with research faculty buildings, student housing, and research offices). Together, the three areas provide five hectares of new public open space—well over a third of the total development area. The three public spaces are an organizing

01

01 (previous)
View of the Marine Basin and University Center on a summer day: an urban "beach" for sunbathing and recreation is supported by adjacent café kiosks and residences

02
University City master plan showing street layout and location of three major public spaces

03
A series of plan diagrams showing proposed FAR, use-type, circulation, and district parking strategies

framework for the plan, connecting the site with new developments on the Eastern Docks, the historic arsenal building, and the city at large. The same three spaces also relate University City's shops, cafés, and apartments with the university's faculty buildings and research facilities at the plan's core.

University City Amsterdam would be developed by the University City Corporation, a governing board composed of members from city government, national government, and the university. Public streets and rights-of-way in the master plan would be maintained by the city. All lots, including the public parks, would be managed by the University City Corporation. Housing and commercial lots would be leased for 99 years to development partners; the revenues would fund site improvements, parks, and part of the construction costs of the university itself. This framework could produce well-funded, programmed, and maintained public space for the city and allow the public university, over a 100-plus-year time frame, the flexibility and future capital to expand and extend its core mission.

04

(05)

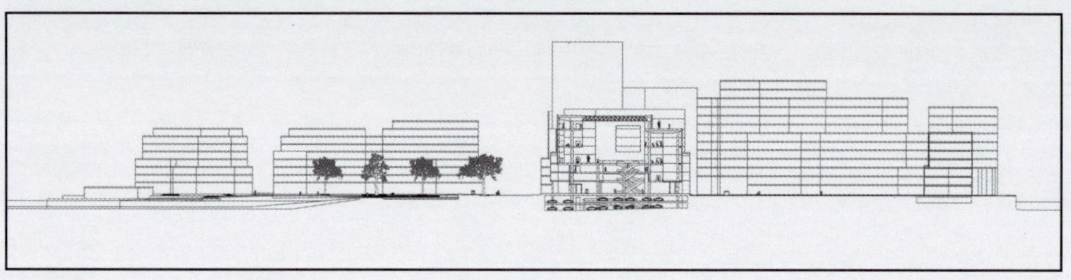

(06)

04 (previous)
Nighttime view of the Marine Basin and University Student Center in winter: with ice-skating and a holiday market

05
Bird's-eye view of the Etablissement Park

06
North-south section through the University Student Center and the Marine Basin

07
Views of the Etablissement Park showing daytime recreation and an evening concert on the green

07

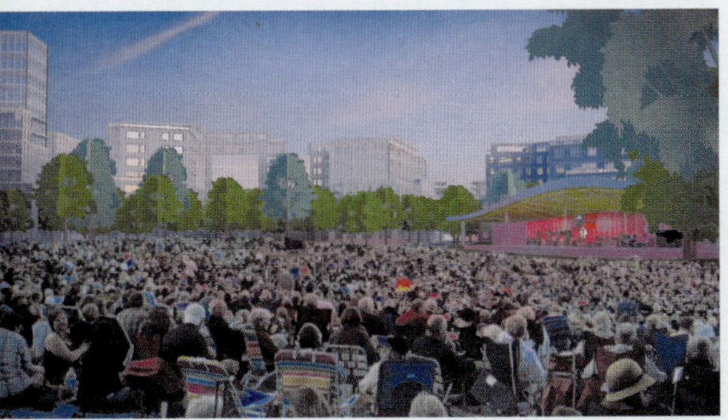

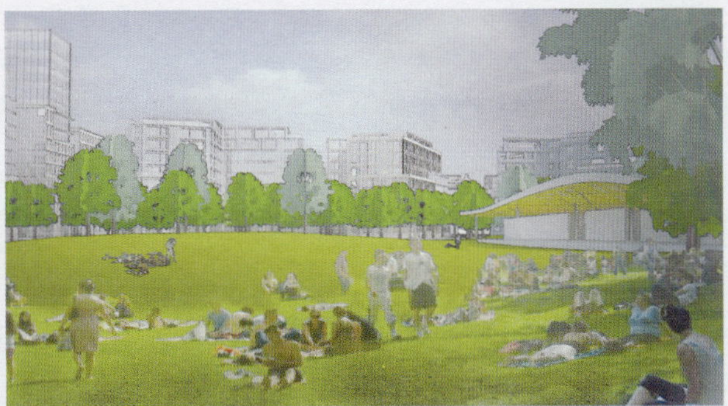

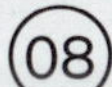

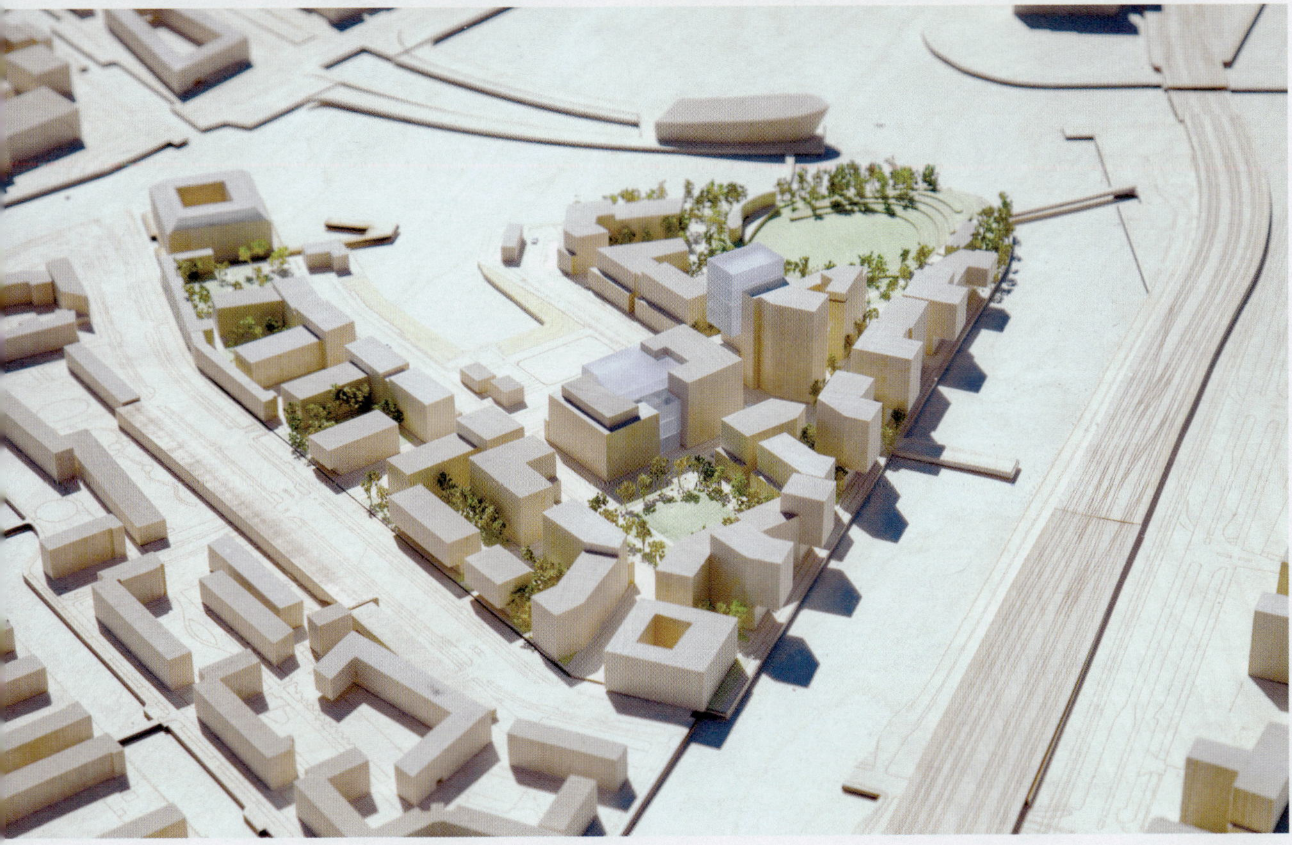

08

08
Site model showing central Amsterdam, southwest of the site

09 (overleaf)
Aerial perspective of the University City master plan

09

Todd Christensen, Athletic Peninsula

The Athletic Peninsula is a sports-oriented development that is meant to change the way Amsterdamers live, play, and perceive their city. Modern-day society loves sports and recreation, and the number of people tuning in to watch major competitive events increases every year. Sports have always brought together large, diverse groups, and, today, their reach is further than ever. Professional sports teams are a valuable marketing tool that can solidify a city's identity, generate revenue, and attract new residents. Major events, such as the Olympic Games or the World Cup, have provided so much stimulus that, in some cases, they have completely rebooted an urban center or, in preparation for an event, created from scratch a piece of the city. For example, the 2012 London Olympics was the most-watched event in the history of television, and, in 2022, Qatar will be hosting the World Cup with an estimated budget of $220 billion. Sports have evolved into something more than recreation; they are now a way that we bond culturally and socially. The aim of the Athletic Peninsula is to tap into this global interest not simply with a sports arena for periodic events but with a series of competition, training, and recreation facilities that will sustain year-round activity at the site.

The Athletic Peninsula will redefine the landscape of Amsterdam, creating a destination for locals, all residents of the

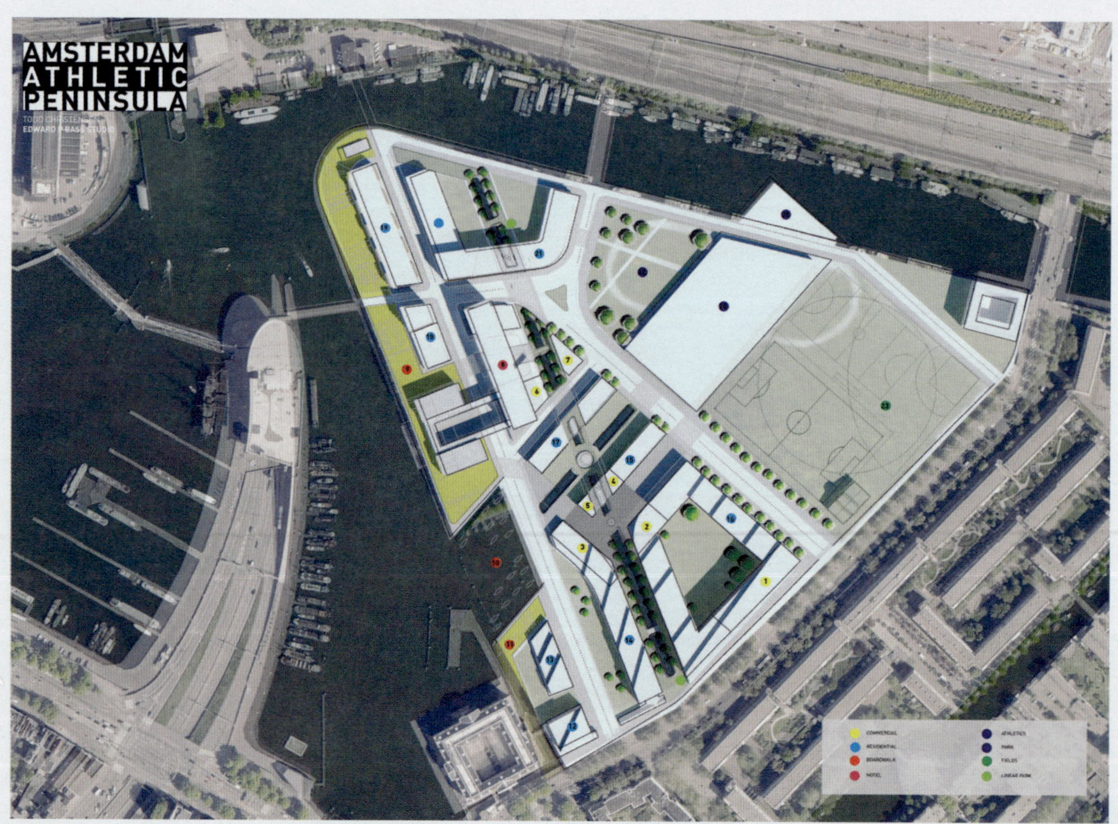

(01)

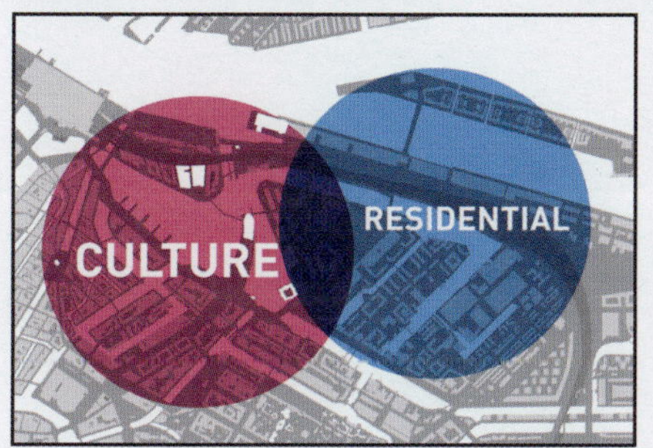

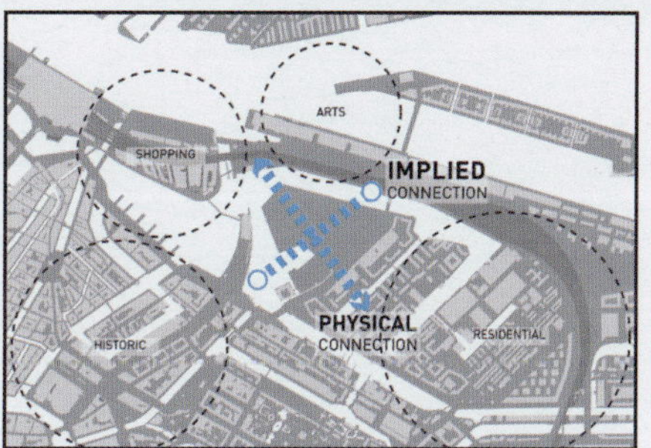

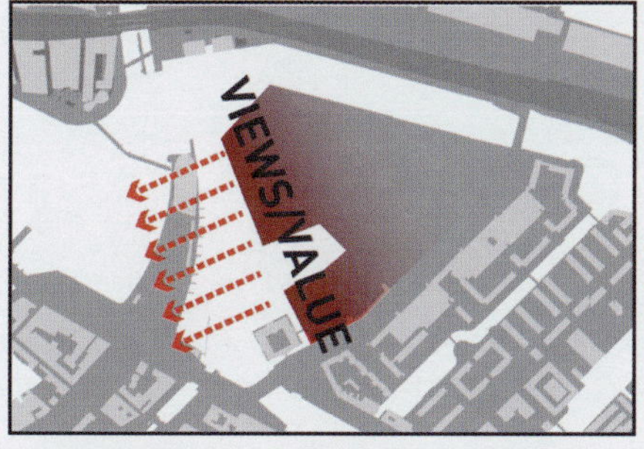

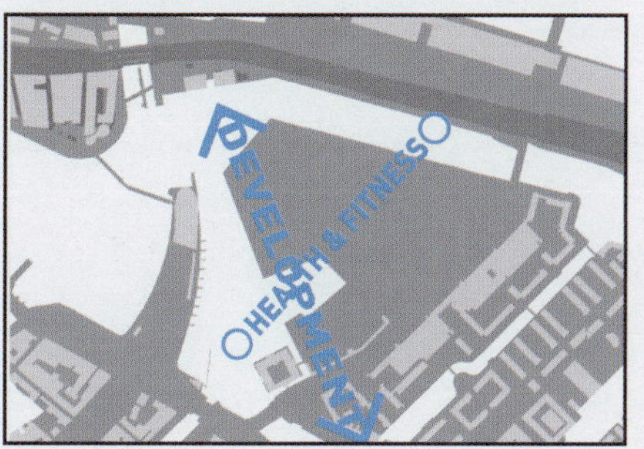

03

01
Master plan of the Athletic Peninsula showing waterfront promenade at left and recreation and training facilities at right

02
View of residential blocks along the linear park

03
Site analysis diagrams

04 (overleaf)
View of the waterfront promenade and residential complex looking southeast with the NEMO science center at left

04

Netherlands, and tourists. Its focus will be on key Dutch sports, such as speed skating and football (soccer). The project contains outdoor practice fields and one of the largest indoor recreational facilities in the country, increasing by ten times the amount of the athletic-related programming within the city limits. The master plan integrates the athletic facilities with affordable housing and a walkable residential component to create a permanent "Olympic Village-like setting within Amsterdam. The site is divided into four quadrants by two axes,

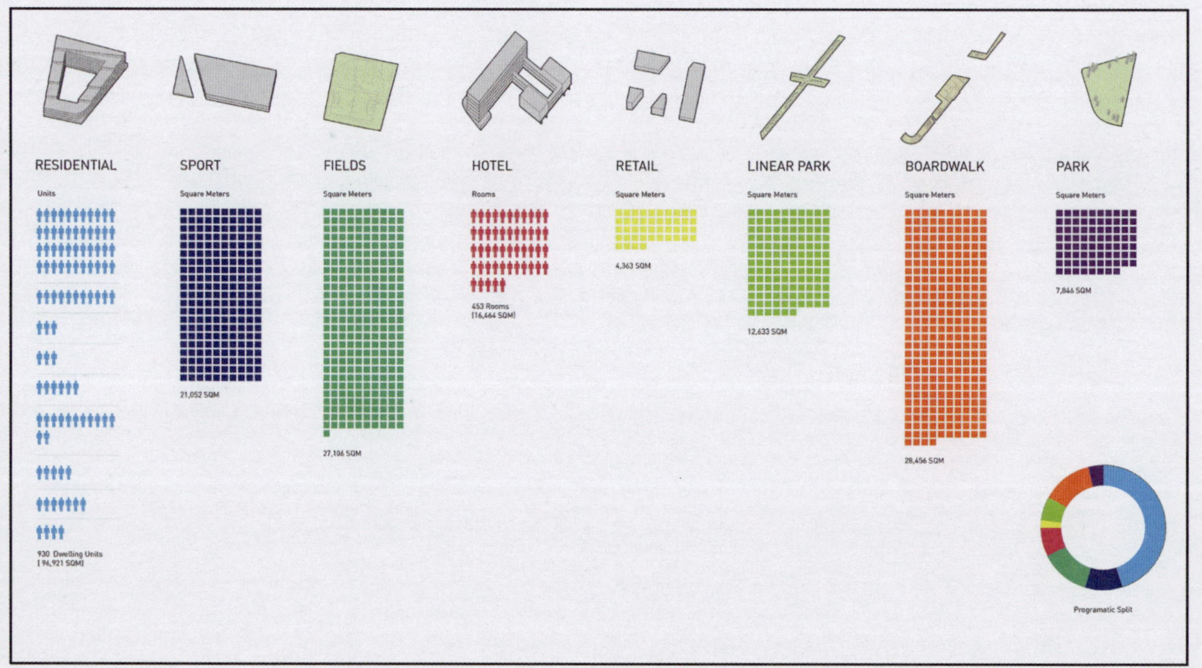

05
Programmatic use breakdown of the Atheletic Peninsula

06
Infrastructure quantity breakdown of the Athletic Peninsula

07
North-south section cut through the waterfront and the linear park

with each axis acting as an anchor for either the residential or athletic program. The vertical axis is anchored by the linear park, which runs the length of the site. The linear park roughly separates the living area from the athletic area. The four quadrants comprise the Waterfront Quarter, offering a hotel, a boardwalk, and high-end apartments; the Park Quarter, comprising a park and market-rate housing in a more secluded portion of the site; the Historic Quarter, located next to existing Maritime Museum and preserving remnants of the site's original historic structures; and the Athletic Quarter, providing views and more affordable housing units as well as quick access to the playing fields.

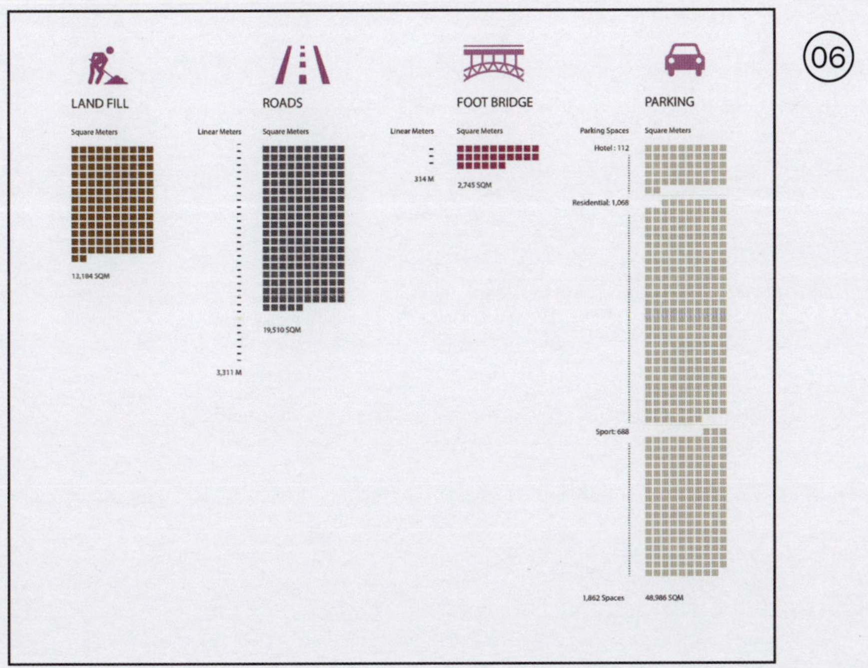

06

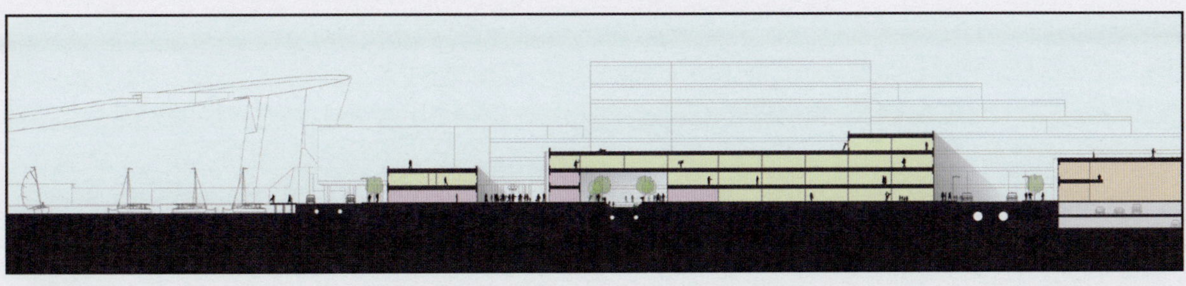

07

Mathew Suen, De Nederland

For centuries, the Marine Etablissement site has existed in the heart of Amsterdam as a blank area on a map—known about, but unseen and unused by the general public. As a part of national defense, its status as a secure location has meant that the public rarely ever gets to see it; despite its public location, it is mostly overlooked by most Amsterdammers. A radical new master plan for the Marine Etablissement must captivate the public, entice a developer, and weather the politics. De Nederland takes its

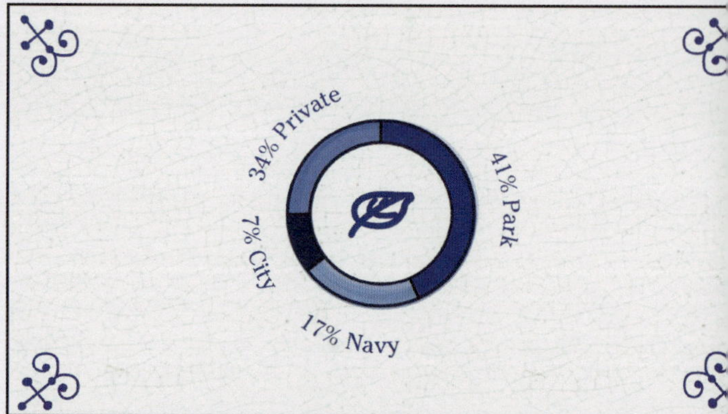

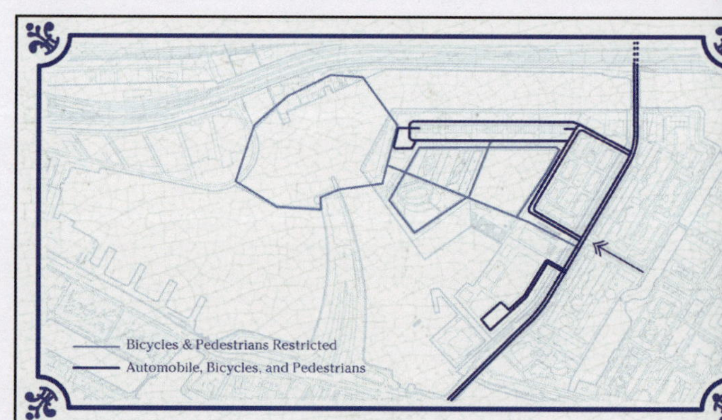

01

01
Site diagrams showing disposition of public and private space as well as primary circulation networks

02
Master plan for De Nederland showing centrally located green space, with waterfront recreational facilites and a row of town houses at the northern side of the site

cues from historic urban planning strategies employed throughout the Netherlands. The core idea is egalitarian: to give the public back the public realm.

Amsterdammers have always flocked to the city's famed canals, which provide a public space for interaction and engagement. The canal to the Dutch is what the street is to any other nation. Thus, this scheme gives back to the city as a public park the section of water that was filled in during the construction of the IJ Tunnel. The rest of the site, which has always existed as a naval base, would be used for private development. The designed permutation here offers the majority of the site for residential units of various types. Economic conditions do not favor high concentrations of retail or commercial space at the farthest extremes of the site. The image of the Netherlands is presented as a kitsch interpretation of various Dutch artifacts, from polders, canals, and dikes to the Delft porcelain houses that can be bought from the many gift shops that line the historic quarters of Amsterdam.

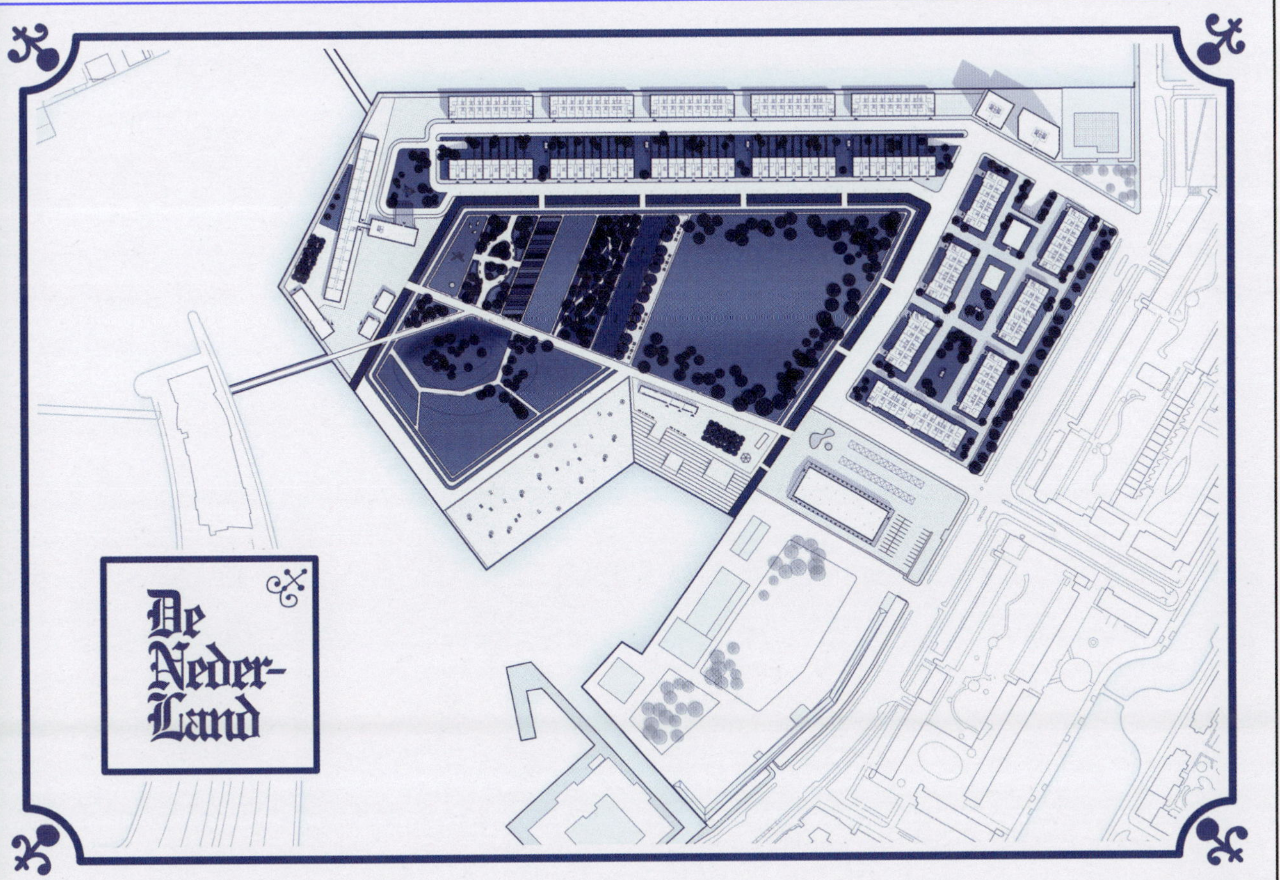

(02)

03

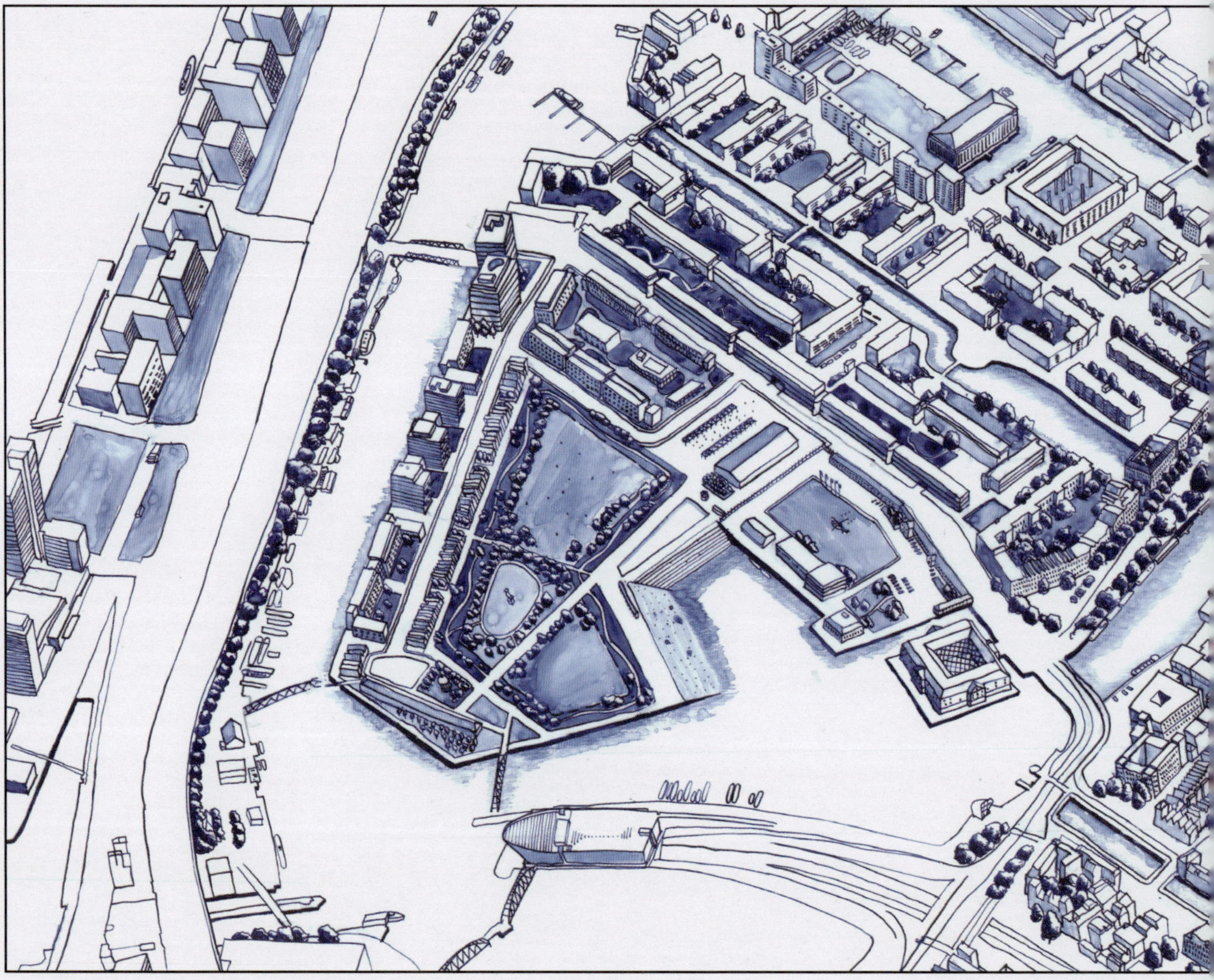

03 (previous)
Aerial perspective looking northeast from central Amsterdam

04
Axon sketch of De Nederland in context, with the NEMO science center and Central Harbor at bottom

05
Components of the master plan, with FAR and GFA allocated to each subsection of the site

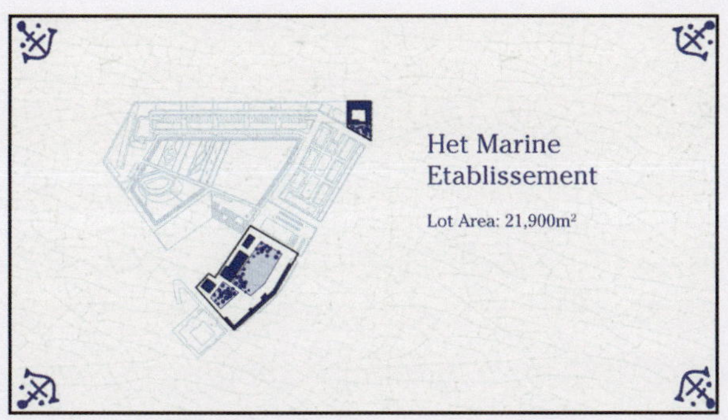
Het Marine Etablissement
Lot Area: 21,900m²

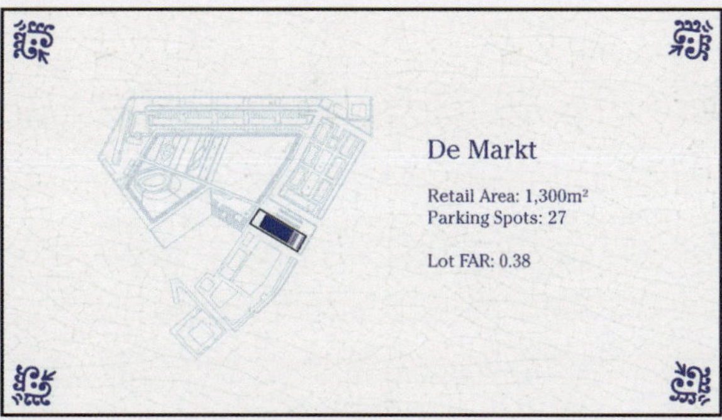
De Markt
Retail Area: 1,300m²
Parking Spots: 27
Lot FAR: 0.38

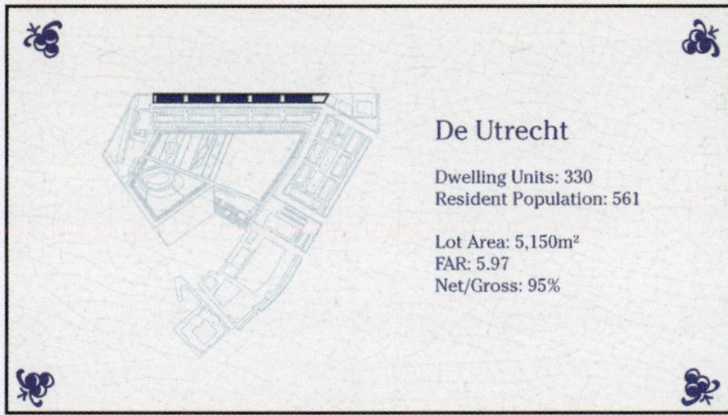
De Utrecht
Dwelling Units: 330
Resident Population: 561
Lot Area: 5,150m²
FAR: 5.97
Net/Gross: 95%

Het Amsterdam
Dwelling Units: 125
Resident Population: 198
Lot Area: 7,851m²
FAR: 1.53
Net/Gross: 89%

Den Haag
Dwelling Units: 312
Resident Population: 493
Lot Area: 13,950m²
FAR: 1.74
Net/Gross: 91%

De Rotterdam
Dwelling Units: 156
Resident Population: 208
Lot Area: 1650m²
FAR: 6.89
Net/Gross: 86%

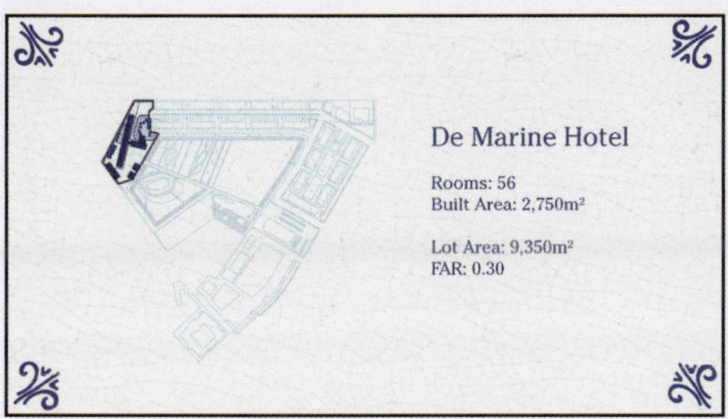
De Marine Hotel
Rooms: 56
Built Area: 2,750m²
Lot Area: 9,350m²
FAR: 0.30

Het Groene Hart
Greenery: 25,800m²
Paved Plaza: 2,500m²
Beach Area: 4,100m²
Area: 52,550m²

05

Miron Nawrtil, NieuwStedelijkCentrum

The Marine Etablissement is the last blank-slate site available for development in central Amsterdam. While not eschewing the benefits of commercial development, this scheme puts a premium on urbanistically and civically responsible development. The proposal's centerpiece is the NieuwStedelijkCentrum, a civic-center complex that comprises the city hall, an opera house, and a ballet theater. The complex also includes a public waterfront that faces Amsterdam and, through a network of boardwalk bridges, connects to the city and the institutions that are concentrated around the navy yard: the Conservatory of Music, the Central Library, the NEMO science center, the maritime museum, and ARCAM. Finally, Amsterdam's StedelijkCentrum, an aging, Post-Modernist eyesore that houses the existing city hall and opera house, would be demolished, allowing its valuable site to be repurposed for revenue-generating housing, thus providing funding for improvements at the new site.

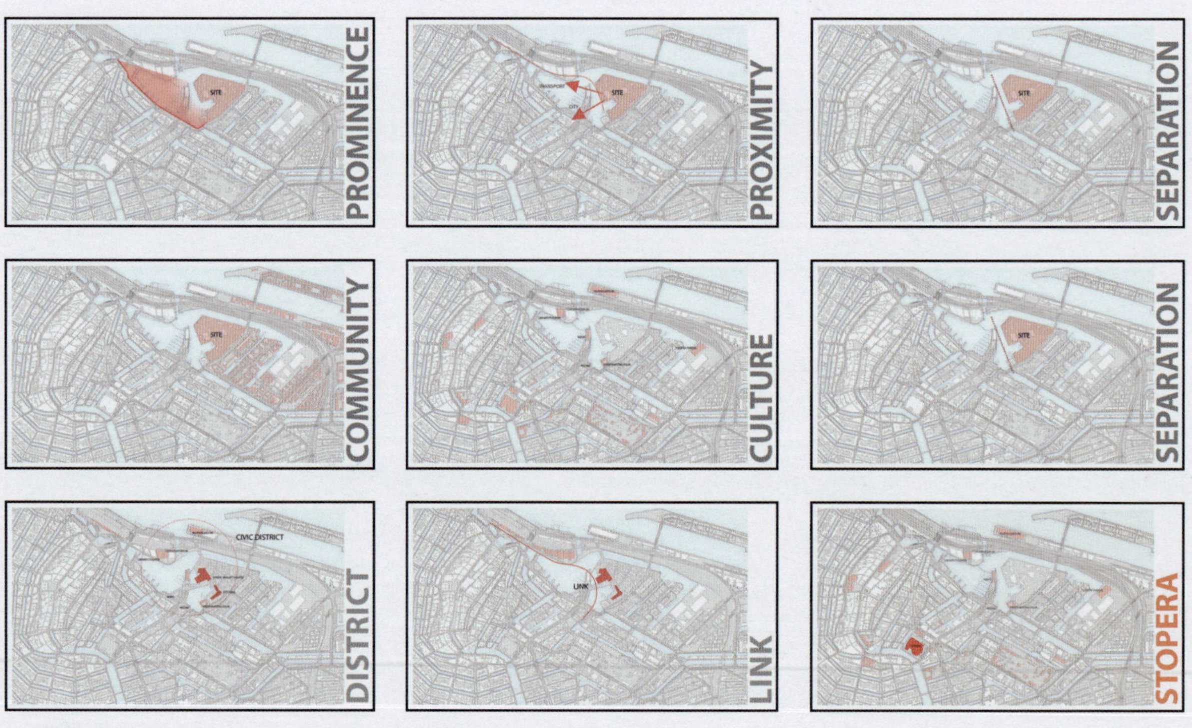

01

02

01
Program analysis diagrams

02
Aerial view of central Amsterdam showing the NieuwStedelijk-Centrum, which will house the new city hall and opera house, and the in-fill development of the old Stedelijkcentrum at the Marine Etablissement site

03

The NieuwStedelijkCentrum scheme is divided into two zones: the public waterfront and the residential neighborhood, which are separated by a public park. Occupying the northern half of the site, the residential neighborhood provides a backdrop to the civic-center complex as well as a link to the existing neighborhoods that border the eastern edge of the site. Modeled on Amsterdam's famous canal zone, the residential layout features weaving, tree-lined streets linked by canals, creating an intimate, park-like environment.

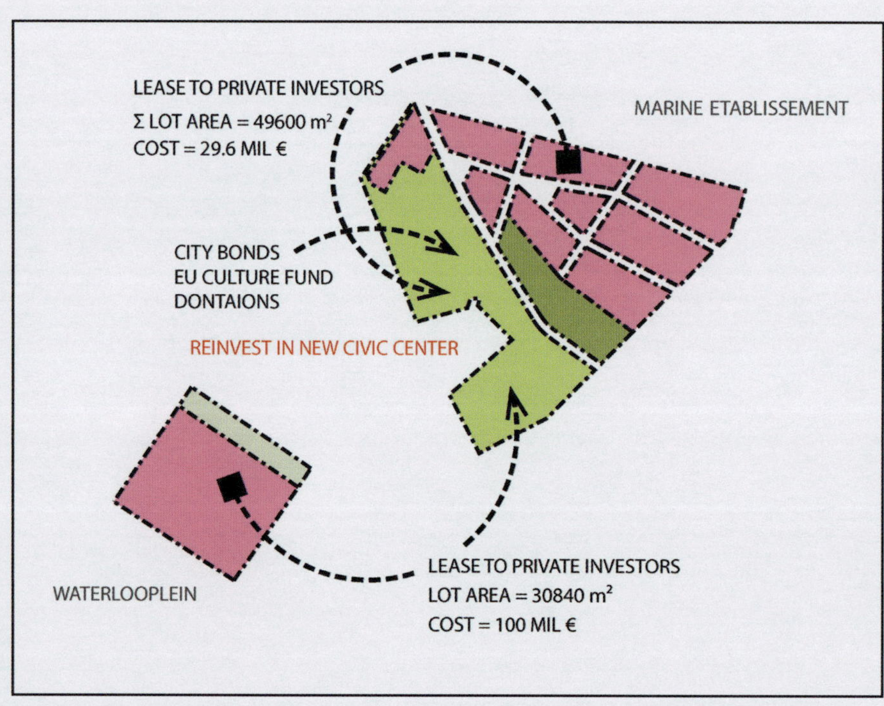

(04)

03 (previous)
Aerial perspective showing the opera house and civic center with a pedestrian bridge connecting the Marine Etablissement with central Amsterdam

04
Concept diagram showing the meta-strategy: shift civic center from Waterlooplein to the Marineterrain site (green), offsetting cost of relocation and improvement with revenues from residential development (pink)

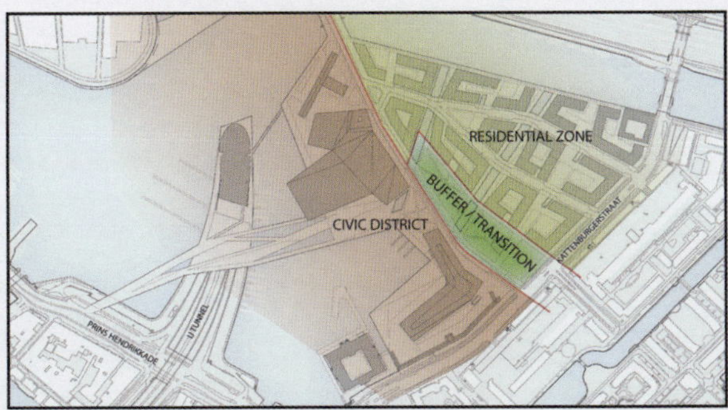

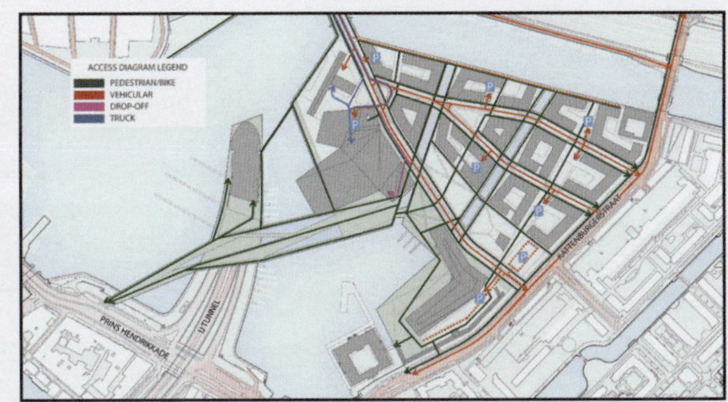

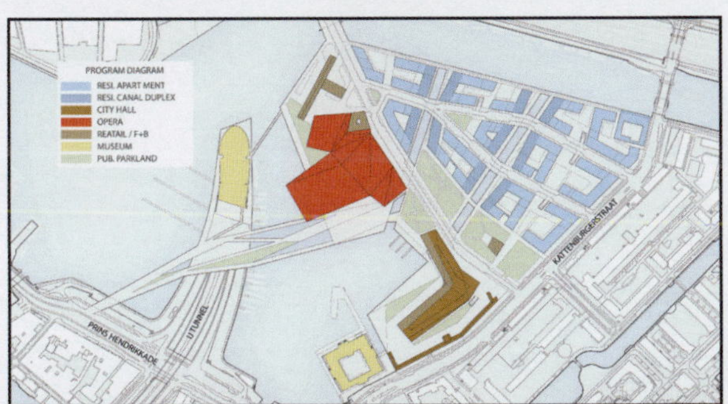

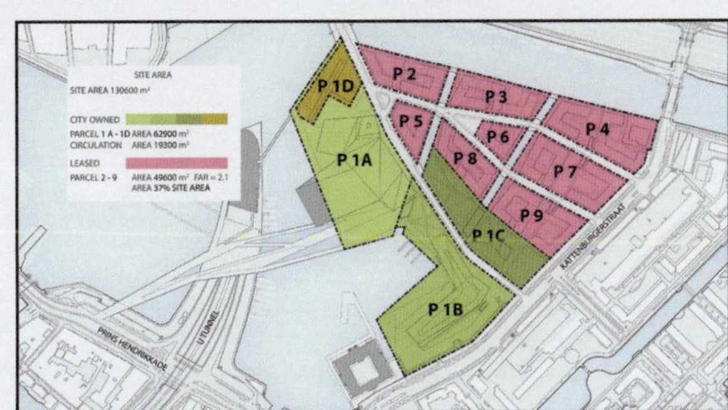

05

06

05
Site diagrams showing civic and residential areas, circulation networks, land use, and zoning strategy

06
Aerial rendering of the NieuwStedelijk-Centrum looking northwest

08

07
Perspective view from the residential neighborhood looking across the new public park toward the opera house and central Amsterdam

08
Perspective view of opera house from the new civic center, with the NEMO science center in the background at left

Jaeyoon Kim, Accelerator

The Accelerator proposal repurposes the Marine Etablissement site as a privately and publicly sponsored think tank or consortium for new ideas and initiatives related to art, design, technology, and the "maker industry." By renovating and expanding two existing buildings on the site, the new innovation building provides unique open-plan co-working and exhibition spaces for a new generation of Dutch entrepreneurs. Precedents of ateliers for the creative industry can be found in many major cities, and the Accelerator space is modeled on the Y Combinator in San Francisco, the New Lab in Brooklyn, and the Cent Quatre in Paris.

Additionally, a portion of the navy-yard site, given its central but secluded location in Amsterdam, is ideally suited for a residential neighborhood linked together by canals leading to the old harbor. This unique condition offers the developer a lucrative opportunity to build a high-end neighborhood for people who strive for the tranquility of suburban living but the convenience of downtown city life. The idea for the residential neighborhood was inspired by a typological study of Dutch city

(01)

01
Aerial view of the Accelerator project showing adaptive re-use of existing buildings (bottom left in plan) and addition of residential blocks (middle and top of plan)

02 (overleaf)
A residential courtyard within the Accelerator project

02

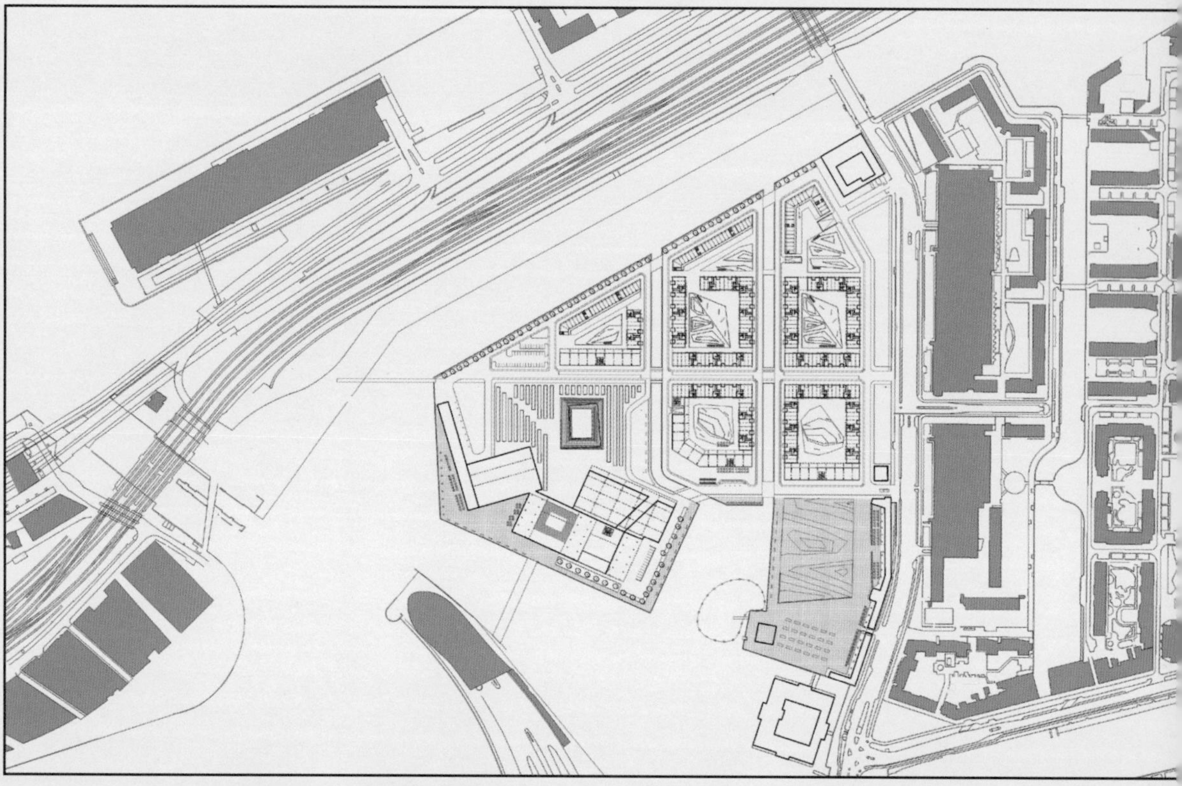

04

03
Site plan of the Accelerator showing residential unit configuration and open-plan “maker” spaces on the site

04
Aerial view of site plan showing phasing of program

blocks and, in particular, canal city blocks. Revenues generated by the development of this new high-end canal neighborhood will partly support the Accelerator. The scheme's detailed staging plan allows for organic development over time. The plan starts with the partial withdrawal of the navy and the establishment of the first phase of the Accelerator in existing naval buildings. Incremental re-purposing of the Marine Etablissement site by new participants in the Accelerator consortium and new residents of the neighborhood will occur over a longer timeframe. Within this solid framework, the strategy allows for a flexibility that can adapt over time to address ever-changing market demands.

06

05
Balconies and terraces within the residential area provide a sense of exterior connection and community

06
Model photograph looking northwest

07 (overleaf)
Aerial rendering looking northeast

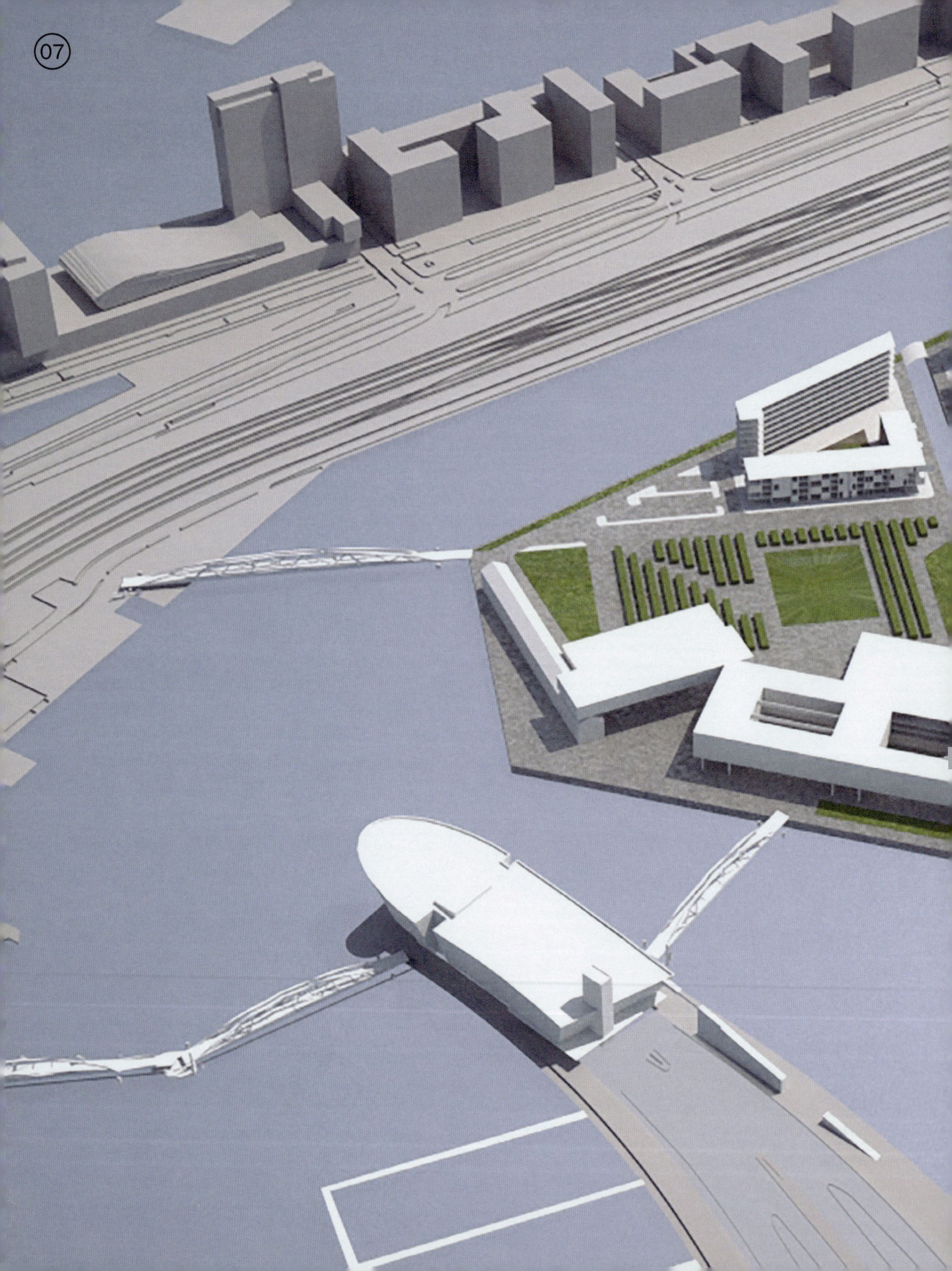
07

Matthew Rauch, Emerald Harbor

Despite the Marine Etablissement's historic importance and prominent location within the City of Amsterdam, the site has remained isolated because of its function as an active naval base. In addition to this programmatic isolation, a series of boundaries have further separated it from the rest of the city, including the railroad tracks to the north, the historic wall to the east, and the NEMO science center and IJ Tunnel to the southwest. As a result of these large-scale infrastructural and spatial structures, the entire Central Harbor district of Amsterdam has the character of leftover space, and does not fully engage the public realm. This master plan for the Marine Etablissement site opens new connections in all directions but also includes the entire Central Harbor district within its scope. A network of pocket parks and pathways lining the harbor links the historic city with newer developments to the north and east and makes the Marine Etablissement site an integral part of the center of Amsterdam.

Because of the site's iconic stature in the city and its close proximity to major international transportation systems and hotel conference facilities, the Marine Etablissement site has the opportunity to become a destination for both locals and tourists. In order to facilitate this vision of Amsterdam as a world-class city,

01

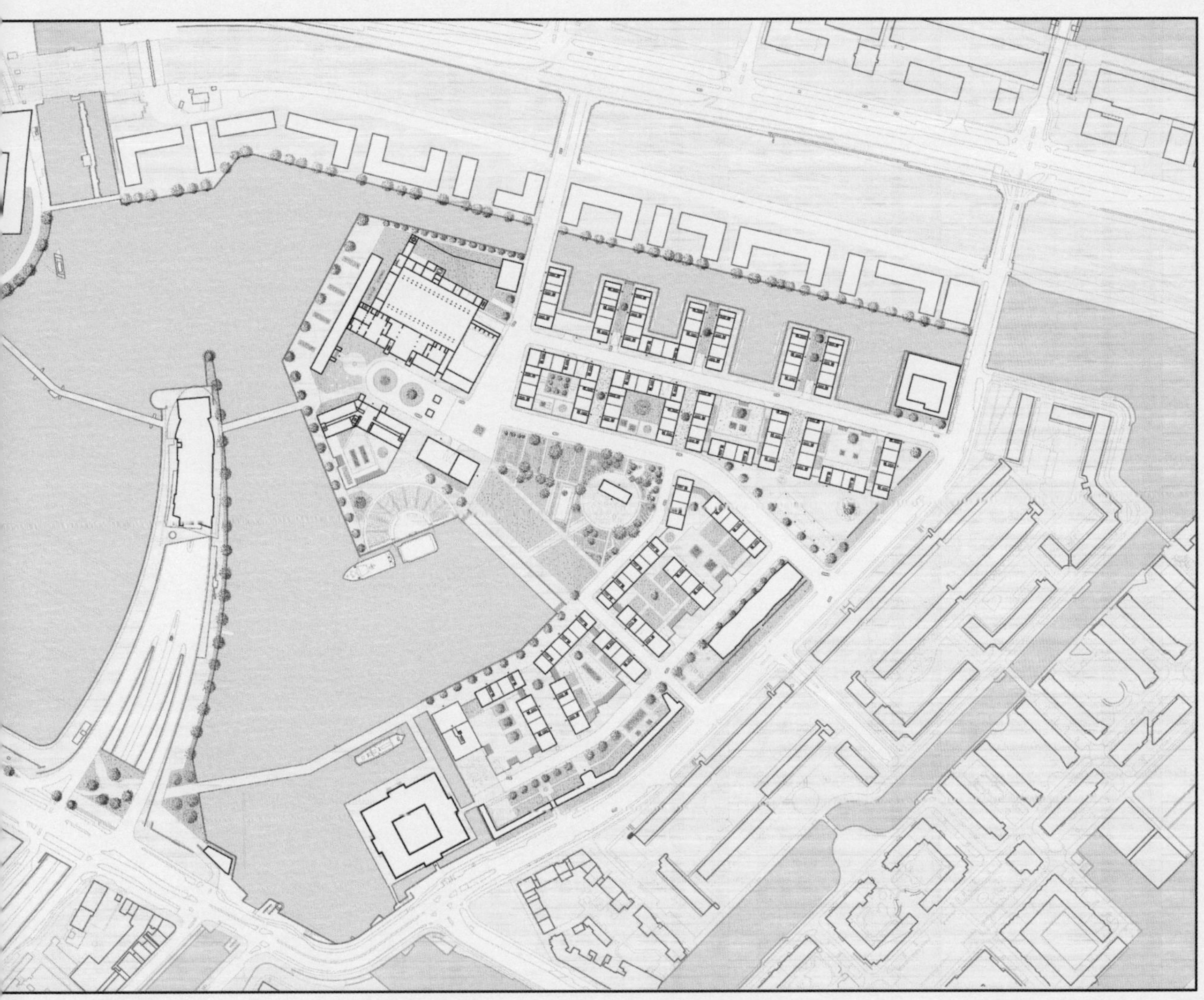

02

01
Site photos of Amsterdam's Central Harbor district: the gray paving along the harbor (left) contrasts sharply with the green vegetation along the historic canals

02
Marine Etablissement site plan showing new uses, including a conference and hotel campus to the northwest, a residential neighborhood to the southwest, and, in the very center, a public park with views back toward the city

the proposal divides the site into three complementary uses. The northwestern portion is appropriated for use as a conference and hotel campus, with the old brick structure, which occupies the corner of the site, renovated into a restaurant with spectacular views of downtown Amsterdam. The new Marine Etablissement Conference Center will accommodate 3,000 people for conferences, providing twice the capacity of the Beurs van Berlage but with a similar, urban-scale footprint.

Occupying a prime location, a 240-room hotel overlooks an amphitheater that frames views of the Maritime Museum and the historic reconstruction of a Dutch East India Company ship, anchored in the harbor. Together with a new bridge that connects to NEMO and the Oosterdokseiland development to the northwest, the hotel, conference center, restaurant, and amphitheater will turn the Marine Etablissement site into an international destination.

The portions of the site not occupied by the conference campus are given back to the city in the form of housing units and a public park. This new residential neighborhood comprises 870 dwelling units, 250

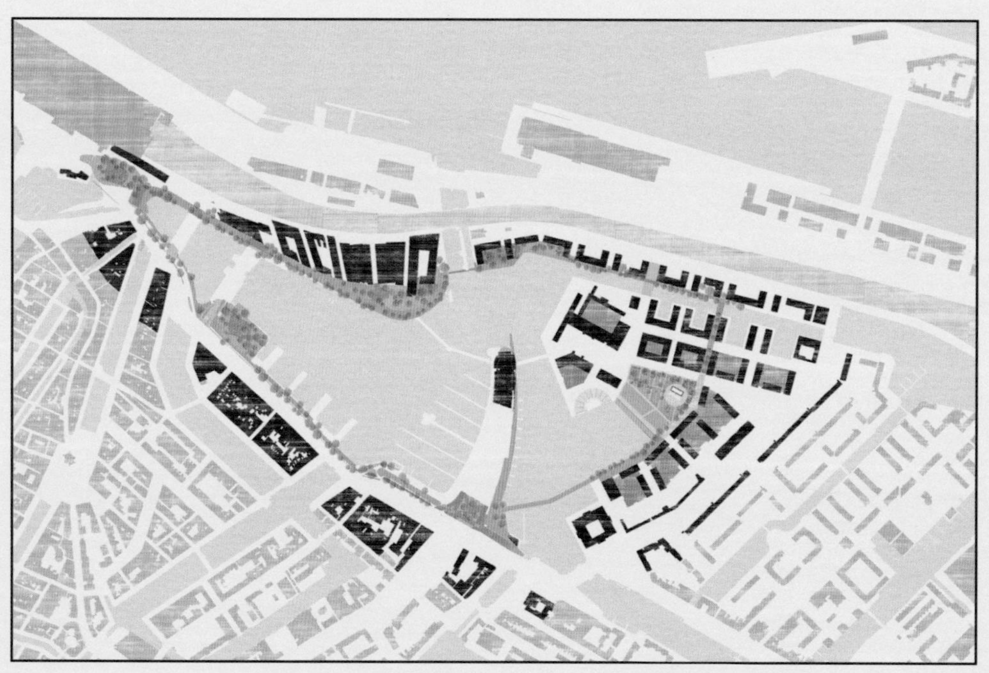

(03)

03
Central Harbor district master plan showing a network of pocket parks and pathways surrounding and uniting the entire harbor, creating an emerald necklace of public space

04
Major barriers isolating the site include the raised railway to the north, the NEMO science center and highway tunnel to the west, and the empty street and housing projects to the east

of which are affordable housing. On this portion of the site, prime housing locations are along the park, where units have views of the park, water, and city. The housing bars immediately behind these structures also have a unique quality, as they open onto the historical structures that frame the site. On the northern shore of the site, a new series of waterways gives residents the ability to park their boat right in front of their dwellings but also provides a view from the houses' courtyards in what would otherwise be the least desirable portion of the site. In addition to the waterways, a phase-two

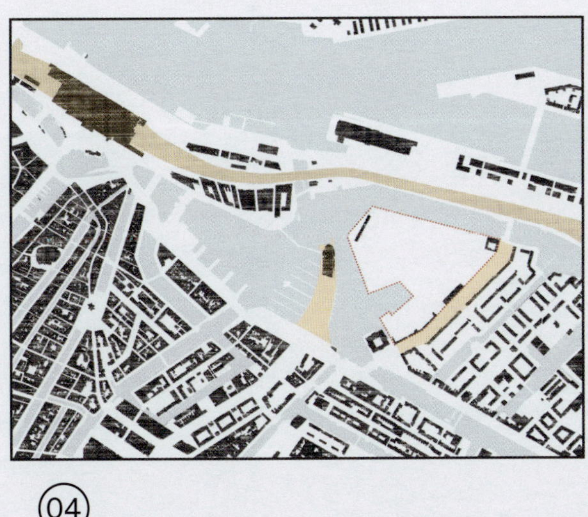

(04)

(05)

05
Existing hotels and conference centers near the train station

06 (overleaf)
Proposed site diagram showing how the Emerald Harbor scheme will open new connections on all sides and make the site a destination

development of housing would be implemented along the railway on the northern portion, not only adding value to the housing along the waterways but also making what is currently a barrier into another one of the many pedestrian-scaled canals for which Amsterdam is famous.

In addition to a master plan for the Marine Etablissement site itself, this proposal considers the development's impact on the entire central district of Amsterdam, which now consists of a number of leftover spaces that lack a distinct pedestrian character. As a way of generating public support for the development, the Marine Etablissement site links with the existing bike path to create an emerald necklace of public parks organized along the water, solidifying the Central Harbor district as a destination, rather than a generic place that merely allows access from the city to the infrastructure along the river. By implementing this vision, the Emerald Harbor project will allow Marine Etablissement site to become a part of the city and the network of spaces that visitors and locals alike know and love.

06

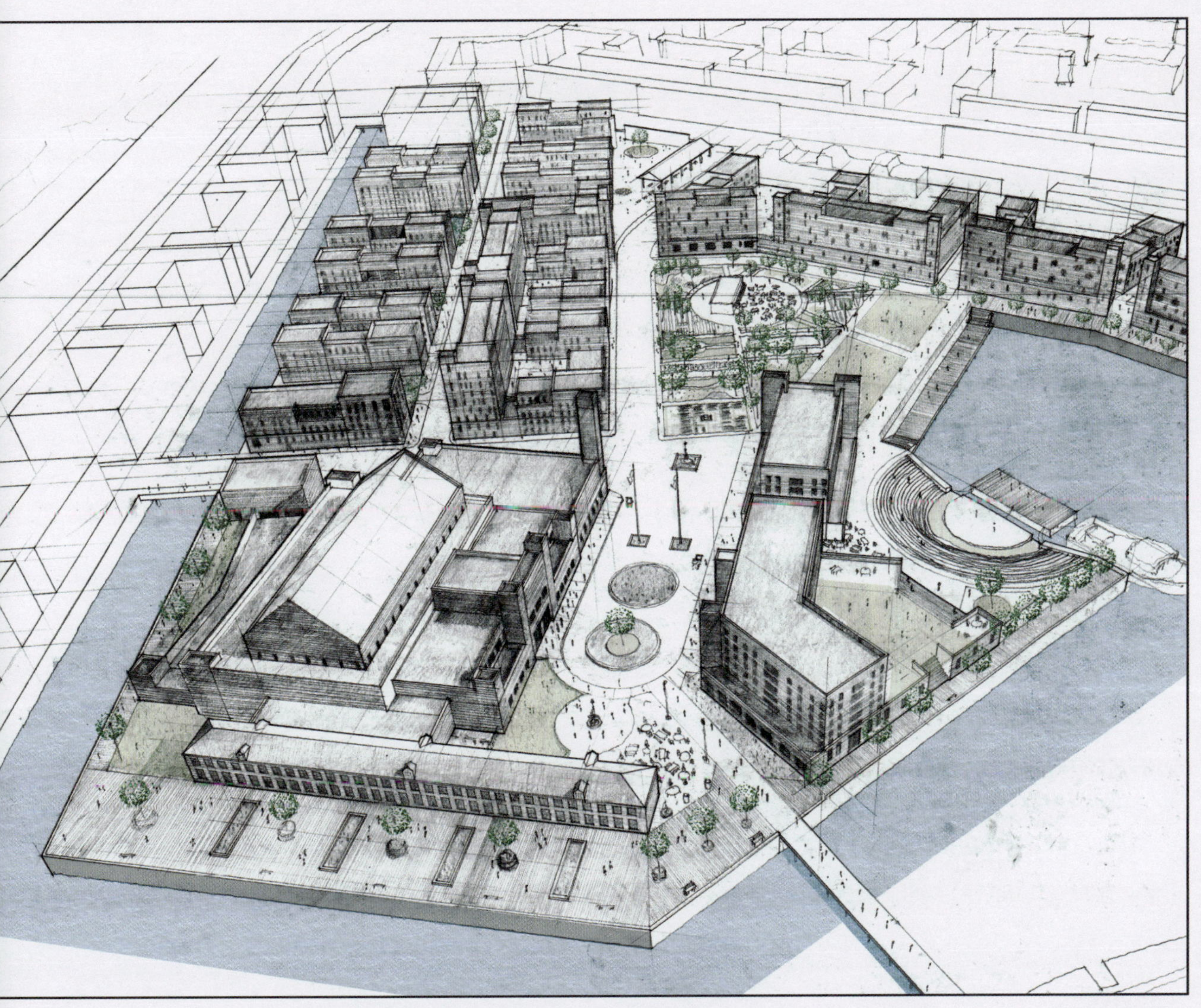

07

07
Aerial view of the proposed Marine Etablissement site. A conference and hotel campus occupies the most prominent portion of the site, with a public park and residential neighborhood given back to the city

08 (overleaf)
Ground perspective showing the Marine Etablissement site from the new city bridge toward the proposed park and the historic Naval Basin

08

04

Late twentieth-century row houses and apartments along the Stokerkade in the Borneo-Eiland section of Amsterdam

The Cha
Property M
Student

lenging
larket and
Response

An Extraordinary Challenge: Europe, the Netherlands, and Amsterdam in 2013: Market Conditions

— Kevin D. Gray, FRICS, Lecturer in the Practice of Real Estate, Yale School of Architecture and Yale School of Management

The fall 2014 Bass studio occurred at an inflection point in the European, and specifically Dutch, property market, making for an interesting case study for a class devoted to the development process. Market considerations are not often a concern for architects as they are for developers, investors, and lenders who take this risk. However, in the Bass studio, the architecture students were encouraged not to ignore either the costs to construct or the value upon completion of their projects, making the studio task especially challenging.

In 2013, commercial real estate markets were generally still in a "workout" stage, recovering from the virtual collapse of the capital and property markets that occurred in 2009–10. Europe's capital markets lagged behind the United States, and, until 2013, it was a painfully slow recovery. By 2012, the volume of commercial property transactions had increased from 2011 by 54 percent in Amsterdam, but prices had increased only 17 percent, as many sales were at distressed prices well below the 2008 peak. Average capitalization rates for all types of commercial property in the Netherlands, according to Real Capital Analytics, increased to 8.4 percent at the end of 2012 from less than 6.5 percent in 2010, representing a major loss in property value. This difficult market was actually a positive for the studio because the demand was low for most commercial uses, land was less valuable than during a boom period, and financing for new development was in short supply. These capital-market conditions favored development with a public component.

On the space-market side, demand for commercial real estate was improving across all sectors, especially in housing, but was still relatively flat. Prices for houses in the Netherlands fell dramatically since a peak in 1999 and had yet to recover.

Powerful demographic forces—a lack of jobs, stagnant incomes, and an increasingly old population, among them—added to the general lack of enthusiasm for new development. In 2013, the major property markets, including office, retail, industrial, multifamily, and hospitality, were all in a very static state, with many newer projects built since 2007 worth less than their cost to construct and their amount of mortgage debt. It seemed as if most of Europe, including the Netherlands, was still in a workout mode as banks sought to find a way to recover lost value after the financial crisis.

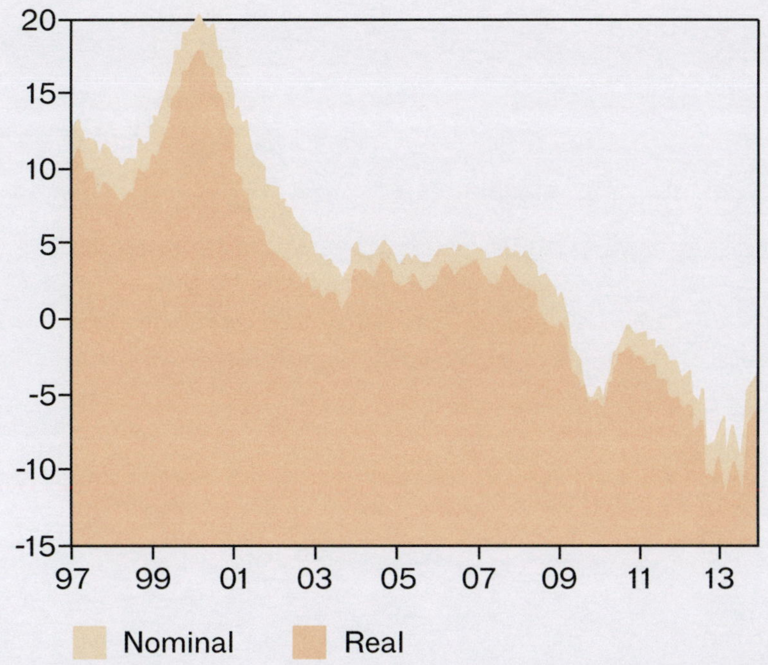

Home Price Changes: Percent Change from Prior Year: 1997–2013

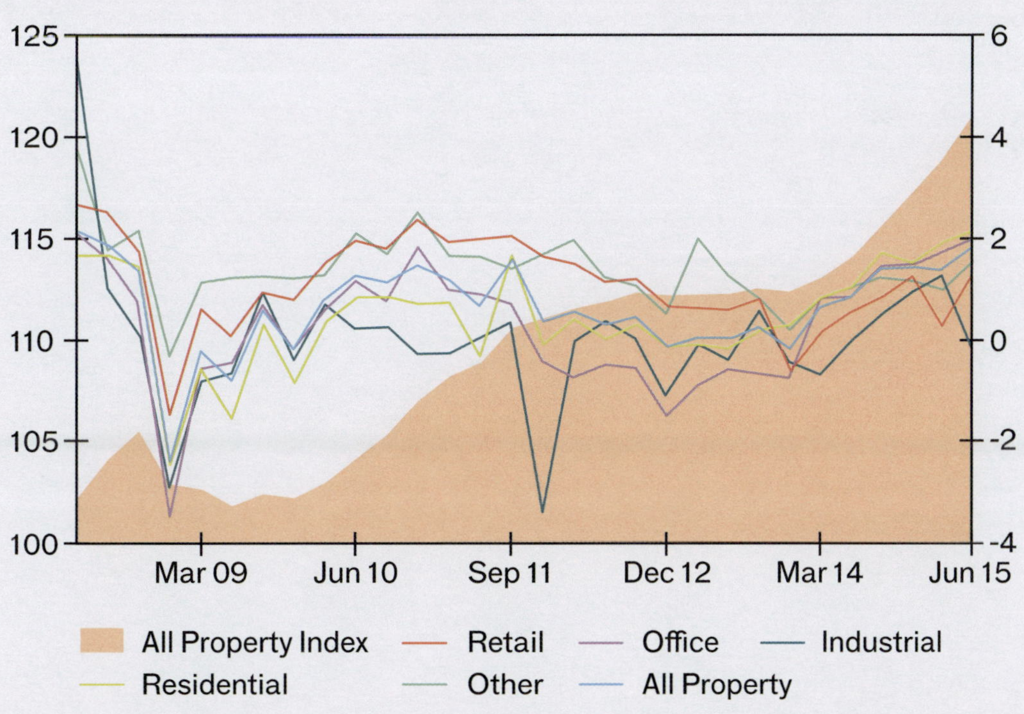

IPD Netherlands Quarterly Property Returns Index, through September 2014

View west across
the Oosterdok:
MAB Development's
Oosterdokseiland
at right

On the supply side, there had been very little new construction in the Netherlands since 2009, and many proposed projects, including those near the Marine Etablissement site, had been postponed or shelved for good. The office market in Amsterdam was essentially static in 2013, according to brokerage firm Savills. Its vacancy rate had held steady at 16 percent since 2006, and average office rents, which had peaked in 2007–08, were at €340 per square meter in 2013, the same level as in 2006. The retail market also remained stagnant, although new retail properties are very limited in the Netherlands and never reached the saturation typical in the United States. Both the supply of retail space and the leasing of space increased, but rents remained essentially flat from 2008 to 2013. There was still continued demand for food retailers in Amsterdam but weaker demand for apparel and home goods, according to CBRE Research. As for hotels and hospitality, Amsterdam continued to attract tourists, mostly on a seasonal basis, and had a relatively constrained hotel supply in the historic center, with very high prices for hotels and many older hotels lacking in amenities. The number of hotels and number of rooms increased in Amsterdam from 2003 to 2010, according to HVS Consulting, with most new hotel rooms added in the four-star category. Revenue per room had also increased steadily, so hotel development was a promising property type in 2013.

Multifamily remained the best property type of all the troubled commercial property types in 2013, but it was hardly reassuring, as house prices continued to remain soft. Social housing is always in short supply, especially for immigrants, the elderly, and those unable to work, but the private housing market was in distress in 2013. Amsterdam is a beautiful, livable city, but not a world gateway city, such as London, New York City, or Hong Kong. It was possible to buy a large, grand canal house in the historic center for less than €1 million in 2013, an extraordinary deal relative to the twelve or so global gateway cities. In this market, even for-sale private housing faced very dim prospects when there were so many bargains available. Average new unit prices in the Netherlands fell slightly from 2012 to 2013 to less than €2,000 per square meter. It is with this very difficult market environment as a backdrop that the Bass studio began its work.

The Student Response

With the studio site located just a short walk from Central Station, the students formulated very thoughtful programs in response to the down market and the site's physical characteristics. Several realized they could take advantage of the site's central location and the weak property values —certainly a moment in time in a cycle—to encourage a public use of the site. Many of these programs have the additional claim of being economic generators, adding employment and creating a multiplier effect for surrounding businesses. Of the nine student projects, all but one had a public aspect, but every proposal incorporated some form of housing to address the housing shortage, the politics of the city, and the relatively better market for housing. The range of proposals by the students was exceptional: Tsai's park design permanently reserves this site for public recreation, which would not be possible if the site had a higher market value; Nawratil's new performing-arts and civic center is a swap of this site with the current Stopera site (the nickname of the opera and city hall, currently combined in one building), an ingenious way to move the city hall closer to the center while freeing up land better suited to residential and retail uses on the Amstel River; Rauch's convention center is much more centrally located and appealing for visitors than the current convention center to the south of the city, at the Amsterdam World Trade Center; Howlett's university complex represents a consortium of Dutch universities on a special campus, including research and hotel facilities, and satisfies a demand for student housing; Barre's observation tower, inspired by the London Eye, generates revenue with a museum complex that includes additional housing, which addresses a need for more affordable studio units; Christensen's public-private sports complex, similar to Chelsea Piers in New York City, addresses the lack of adequate sports and exercise facilities in this part of Amsterdam; H. Kim's artists' colony provides studio and gallery space; J. Kim's incubator generates new technologies and business with a kind of communal housing and would have a multiplier effect on job creation; Finally, Suen's commercial proposal is a dense housing development around a green space, with a mix of rental units.

Development Costs

As a way to evaluate each project, general development costs per square meter were provided by MAB for each student project and included typical construction costs, plus an allocation for developer profit. In addition, the cost of the land, estimated at €80 million, is included as an outright purchase or as a ground lease at 3.5 percent per year. The analysis demonstrated to students that additional canals, bridges, and other infrastructure greatly increase development costs on this relatively small site, as do any specialized amenities, such as museums.

Site and Building Cost Estimates: Marine Etablissement						
Student Architect	Project Major/Minor Component	Site Cost (MM €)	Building Costs (MM €)	Site Costs as a % of Total Costs (Excluding land)	Total Cost Excluding Land (MM €)	Total Costs Plus Land at €80 MM
Barre	Tower/Museum Housing	76.72	553.90	12.2%	630.62	710.62
Christensen	Sports Complex/Housing	370.66	406.61	47.7%	777.26	857.26
Kim, J.	Tech Incubator/Housing	112.19	320.84	25.9%	433.04	513.04
Howlett	University/Housing	213.84	627.17	25.4%	841.01	921.01
Kim, H.	Art Galleries/Housing	343.28	263.34	58.6%	606.62	686.62
Nawratil	Performing Arts/Housing	388.09	449.16	46.4%	837.25	917.25
Rauch	Conference Center/Housing	120.81	717.59	14.4%	838.40	918.40
Suen	Housing/Park	81.26	261.21	23.7%	342.47	422.47
Tsai	Structured Park/Housing	487.56	39.92	92.4%	527.47	607.47
Averages		€243.82	€404.42	37.6%	€648.24	€728.24

Complete costs breakdowns for the projects during the development phase

As shown in the chart above, total project costs varied widely, from €422 million for Suen's commercial housing scheme to €921 million for Howlett's proposed University College. The average project cost for each student scheme was €728 million. The relationship between site and building costs was also markedly different among the student architects: Site costs as a percent of total costs ranged from 12 percent (Barre), when there were fewer canals and less infrastructure, to a high of 92 percent (Tsai) for a structured park proposal that, in its earliest iteration, was almost entirely site costs.

Estimating Market Value

Valuation of the projects is a difficult metric, since there are no effective market-derived capitalization rates for the non-income-producing components of the student projects. How does one put a value on, for example, a park, which increases the quality of life and house values in the neighborhood, or of a university or conference center that has a multiplier effect on business and employment? However, a hypothetical, market-value estimate for each project provided insight for the students, helping them to understand the relative contribution of income in each scheme and the magnitude of any cost shortfall, which would need to be made up in the form of a public subsidy.

Income and Value Estimates: Marine Etablissement						
Student Architect	Project Major/Minor Component	Total Cost Excluding Land Assumed as Ground Rent (MM €)	Estimated Capitalization Rate for Income Components	Estimated Average Unit Prices for Sales of Housing Units (€)	Estimated Project Market Value Using the Income Approach (MM €)	Project Value as a % of Project Cost
Barre	Tower/Museum Housing	630.62	7.0% to 7.5%	135,000	695.01	110.2%
Christensen	Sports Complex/Housing	777.26	6.5% to 8.0%	1,250,000	480.72	61.8%
Kim, J.	Tech Incubator/Housing	433.04	All Sales	900,000	462.70	106.8%
Howlett	University/Housing	841.01	5.25% to 6.5%	All Rental	369.23	43.9%
Kim, H.	Art Galleries/Housing	606.62	All Sales	1,500,000	412.00	67.9%
Nawratil	Performing Arts/Housing	837.25	5.25% to 8.0%	All Rental	206.94	24.7%
Rauch	Conference Center/Housing	838.40	5.25% to 8.0%	All Rental	689.42	82.2%
Suen	Housing/Park	342.47	5.25% to 7.0%	All Rental	139.35	40.7%
Tsai	Structured Park/Housing	527.47	5.25% to 7.0%	NA	123.37	23.4%
Averages		€648.24			€397.64	61.3%

Market value estimates for student projects

In general, capitalization rates were developed based on the low cost of capital at the then-current government-bond rates, as well as the limited data on actual market transactions—often of distressed assets—which occurred in the region in 2012. Capitalization rates for income-producing components range from a low of 5.25 percent for parking garages and 6.5 percent for hotels to 7.75 percent for the viewing tower and 8.0 percent for the sports complex. Paradoxically, in a city known for its walkability, the highest valued use at the time of the studio was for parking. However, since 2013, parking values have dropped substantially as a result of the reduction in private vehicles in the city. Market value in the study had two sources: the sales value of housing units and other interests to be sold at completion and the capitalized value of income components.

As shown in the chart above, project market values range from a low of €123 million for a park with a parking garage and little housing (Tsai) to almost €700 million for Barre's densely developed 200 units of for-sale micro-housing. On average, the nine schemes were worth only 61 percent of the estimated costs. Estimated values of unit sales and ongoing income ranged from only 23.4 percent (Tsai) to 110.2 percent of total project costs (Barre). Only two schemes (Barre and Kim) have estimated market values that exceed—and only by very small amounts—the project costs. The large number of housing units with lower site costs in Barre's and Kim's proposals achieves the surplus of value over cost, although Barre has micro-housing at very affordable rates, while Kim proposes single-family canal houses at the luxury end of the market. Those projects with the greatest deficit of cost over value included the structured park (Tsai), the performing-arts center (Nawratil), and the university college (Howlett). Since these are non-profit uses, deficits for these projects are to be expected.

While it may seem unfair to measure these projects based on their income production, it is the most basic method for measuring their relative value. The value estimates are not intended to be judgments on the quality of individual projects but, rather, serve to raise the level of public awareness and debate on the need for profit versus the need for a park, a performing-arts center, or a university as a public good. Each of these non-profit uses has other potential benefits in the form of increased tourism, retail expenditures, and area property values. The need for public subsidy in the form of bonds, taxes, and other financial sources is not a negative factor. On the contrary, public-private partnerships are often part of European development and are becoming increasingly common for urban projects in the United States. Isn't it worth €1 billion to have a new university, conference center, or performing-arts center for Amsterdam? Is it unreasonable or naïve to expect the income-producing parts of a project to fund the public components, shifting costs for public improvements to private development?

Creativity in Practice

The Bass studio gave our students a great opportunity to wrestle with the issues of cost and value that are usually the responsibility of the developer, the investor, and the lender. It may be years before they face a similar challenge in their own practice. The students rose to the challenge, formulating viable projects—both for profit and non-profit—that very cleverly balanced the demands of a very difficult property market with those of the public. Vision is an important part of the architect's role, especially so when there are many constraints imposed by the market, the site, and the politics of place. What is most intriguing is that no two students developed the same response to the market, the same use, or even the same need for a market-driven solution. Money isn't everything; sometimes, it is simply a means to an end. The role of the creative individual in the development process, as shown by the studio, is a source of optimism that fresh, original thinking will continue to lead the way forward.

View of the docks on the south side of the Marine Etablissement

Desigr
Devel
Two Wor

ers and
opers:
ds Apart?

— Erik Go and Hans-Hugo Smit

How do you teach students to gain insights into the real-world development process and the role of the architect in a development team? The Bass studio simulated some of the working methods that MAB Development has implemented in its projects throughout Europe, applying them to one of the most central sites in Amsterdam, the Marine Etablissement. Through a multidisciplinary approach in which design is a synthesizing tool and different needs were visualized, Yale students were taken step by step through an abridged version of the concept development process. They learned that successful development requires not only great design but also marketability, feasibility, and stakeholder management. They also learned that "good" architects can contribute positively to vital elements of development.

Architecture plays an important role in any MAB project. Selecting the most suitable architects for our projects has resulted in long-term partnerships with established firms, such as Rem Koolhaas, Cesar Pelli, Rob Krier, Massimiliano Fuksas, Gigon & Guyer, and Jakob + Macfarlane. For each project, the decision to work with a specific architect is well-considered. A selection procedure can be carried out successfully only if the development team knows exactly what the architect's brief will be. To facilitate this, MAB has a history of employing, from the very early stages of a project, its own concept architects and urbanists as internal members of the development team that researches feasibility, explores the boundaries of what is possible, and defines the assignment to give to external architects. In short, MAB defines the development concept. Our Concept Group and, later, Studio MAB have developed numerous inner-city concepts that have resulted in the construction of projects such as Oosterdokseiland in Amsterdam, De Resident in The Hague, and City Center in Almere. In the past decade, other disciplines, such as market research and marketing, were added to this team as it became clearer that concept development is a multidisciplinary activity requiring direct and constant input from other professions.

Designing in a Developer's Context

For the purpose of this advanced studio, we asked the students to take on the role of both the architect and the concept developer. This tactic meant that, although the final output of the studio was focused on urban and architectural design, the required input involved much more than that.

The role of the developer is that of a spider in a web. In this position, synthesizing the demands of many different parties requires not only a thorough understanding of these parties and their motives but also the skills to define common ground and the creativity to find feasible solutions. In real life, this process involves intense cooperation with many different stakeholders, including designers, technical consultants, users, politicians, financiers, investors, and so on. In this simulation, we focused, for practical reasons on the market and the urban context.

So, what does it mean to work as an architect or designer in this context? Not many architects will end up in a position in which they are both the designer and the developer. However, many of those trained to be an architect will have to deal with developers on a day-to-day basis. Architects—and, in this case, those who work specifically as a developer—have the unusual ability to visualize concepts and make them comprehensible to a multidisciplinary team. Especially in the very early stages of development, this talent helps the team to quickly understand the consequences of different viewpoints and, therefore, work more efficiently. Thus, at this stage, design is more of a synthesizing tool than an end product. Although using design as a communication tool between different disciplines places it—and its designer—right at the center of the development process, it does not necessarily make architecture or design the leading factor of a project. Working within a developer's context, architects need to understand, accept, and embrace this reality if they want to maximize their added value.

This notion is substantially different from the concept of the architect as a creator and requires a different skill set. Next to the traditional creative, technical, and aesthetic skills, an understanding of the market, the socio-political context, and the economics of real estate development needs to be an essential part of the designers tool kit. Insight into this complex process and the required skills to operate as a designer were perhaps the most ambitious learning objectives of this studio.

New Ways To Define Quality

In today's new reality, real estate development in the Netherlands and northern Europe is not primarily about adding more space but adding better space. While "more" is about quantity—and, basically, a matter of building—"better" is about quality. Quality in real estate development is not just the architect's domain. Even if "quality" is defined in only spatial or aesthetic terms, other parties involved in the process also should have a say. Quality has many more dimensions, including utility, stability, sustainability, and marketability. This last dimension borders the notion of market quality, which centers on catering to customer needs and looking at the earning potential of a scheme. Doing what the market wants and striving to deliver market quality are often deemed populist, right-wing, and, therefore, reprehensible.

But market quality should also be a shared concern. Indeed, market quality is by no means new to architects or architectural training. The human aspect of architecture and urban design forms a large part of the curriculum in many schools. But does this really provide the necessary skills to analyze what people want and what they value? And, if so, how does this extrapolate into design? No one would question that architects are skilled at translating (human) processes into relationship diagrams and spatial requirements, occupancy into surfaces, and climate conditions into building skins to form an efficient, sustainable building. That is what people physically need. But what do people want?

In our cooperation with architects and urban designers, we see far too often that this aspect of market quality is not taken seriously enough. Fixed ideas—often shaped by a personal design aesthetic and not necessarily supported by empirical research—prove hard to counter. The inevitable discussion about the need for individual commercial expression versus a homogenous building appearance is but one example of this.

In order for new schemes to be successful, all parties involved should strive for market quality. Therefore, all parties should learn to develop an in-depth knowledge of the qualitative needs and wishes of consumers. A recent discussion MAB had regarding the appropriateness of adding private external spaces—that is, balconies and terraces—to buildings in the center of Amsterdam illustrates the need for this level of understanding. Research shows that balconies are seen as "quality" architecture by consumers, and their absence, in some cases, becomes a disqualifier. This data appeared to be in conflict with the more abstract notion of the qualities of the historical façade and how new buildings fit in that context. It finally resulted in a sensitive design solution that optimized both qualities. We need to actually listen to what people want. How do people want to use space? What do they value in a building or in an area? How can a plan and design help to capture that value?

New Worlds

Defining what people want is difficult, especially in these highly dynamic times in which qualitative demand for offices, shops, housing, and other

A view of canal houses and apartments built as part of Amsterdam's Java-eiland development in the 1990s

real estate seems to be changing quickly. The new world of work requires different workplaces, with flexible office concepts in central locations. Moreover, people want to work outside the office: they want to work at home, on the road, at Starbucks, or in a hotel lobby. For many, the city has become the office. The new world of retail is not just about e-commerce but also about the impact that new channel has on existing brick-and-mortar shops and shopping areas. These traditional retail environments can survive only if we make the change from good "places to buy" to good "places to be." The housing market is somewhat different because (it could be argued) there are still shortages there. But we see a distinct shift in the qualitative needs of the housing market. The Dutch demographic structure is changing: the population is aging, and single-person households are growing. Moreover, housing needs are changing because of political and fiscal changes. All this leads to a qualitative change in housing demand.

These trends seem to favor central, urban locations, and that is good news for the Marine Etablissement site, which is centrally located in an urban environment. Fundamentally, any long-term development scheme needs a certain amount of flexibility because people have wants that are constantly changing. So, how did this Bass studio capture both the huge market potential as well as the need for flexibility in their designs for the Marine Etablissement site?

Looking at the Marine Etablissement Site

Since the studio was only a couple of months long and the students visited Amsterdam for just one week, getting the right market insight was nearly impossible. For example, some students proposed parking or certain housing typologies that are not traditional in the Dutch market. However, from the start, most students considered a programmatic mix for their scheme that would not only suit the location but also would meet the current market demand. This approach explains, for example, the high residential component in most schemes. Also, programs for sport venues, conference facilities, micro-housing units, a large tourist attraction, and a technology incubator were commendable strategies for filling a gap in the Amsterdam market. In this sense, Owen Howlett's University City may have been the most demand-oriented scheme, given the current buzz in Amsterdam for creating a new university—for which the Marine Etablissement site is actually being considered!

Most students also tried to add market qualities and public spaces. To increase the attractiveness of the site, many students from the outset included parks, waterfront boardwalks, new waterways, or crucial new connections to downtown Amsterdam. In many preliminary sketches, the best sites and views were reserved for public buildings, rather than housing. During the course of the studio, housing moved away from the noisy railroad tracks to the more attractive, south-facing side, a gesture that, from a residential market point of view, was definitely an improvement.

Students faced other challenges, including the notions of temporary use, staging, and working with a flexible framework, as opposed to master-planning. Today, it may seem almost mainstream in the Netherlands to talk about organic development and small-scale private developments. The reworking of former MAB projects as a response to new market conditions—such as the Binckhorst, in The Hague, or the Nieuwstraat, in Arnhem—are examples of this. Both were large, urban redevelopments that evolved into a cluster of smaller developments. The first developments of this approach have now been realized, some more successful than others.

The images of the projects shown in this book illustrate only a fraction of what the students did during the studio. They do not show the intense discussions, laborious calculations, and numerous permutations that preceded these drawings. The output may be elaborately rendered urban architectural plans, but the input was just as elaborate, if not more so. The overall assignment was difficult and complex—possibly too complex to carry out in such a short time. Therefore, the proposals are not as advanced on a design level as some would have wanted. Having said that, as a learning experience, it came as close to real life as it could. This is the setting in which at least some of these young architects will have to operate. For us, it was enriching to be questioned about the things we often take for granted and to be exposed to new and surprising ideas that, in their freshness, could shape our future living environment.

05

Rooftop view from the NEMO Science center at the Marine Etablissement site (left) and the Lands Zeemagazijn

The

Transfor

a Nav

Agile
nation of
Yard

Next Steps for the Navy Yard

—Liesbeth Jansen and Maarten Pedroli

Most things in the world are continually changing. In the process of transforming sites—such as the Marine Etablissement, Amsterdam's navy yard—accommodating these often unpredictable changes is one of the major challenges in real estate development today.

The Marine Etablissement has a proud history. It was the place from which the oceans were explored, new continents were discovered, and worldwide commerce was initiated. It was where the seeds were planted for the Dutch golden age, when Holland was one of the world's most powerful nations, flourishing both economically and culturally. How society views these advancements over time depends, of course, on changing values. Constant over time is the common pursuit of knowledge, innovation, and wealth, driven by people's curiosity and their desire to improve their lives.

Today's accelerating speed of change makes it impossible to predict what specific functions will be needed in the future. Rather than the mere planning of spaces and uses, a resilient development scheme is based on the site's existing qualities, including its history, and optimizes the site's physical potential. Temporary use can be an important instrument to test and enhance those qualities in the short term, before choosing a definite development direction.

The historic gate hermetically sealed the site from the rest of the city

Framework for Development

The navy yard is centrally located in the historic heart of Amsterdam on over 15 hectares that are potentially priceless. So far, market forces have had no role to play here. As a military base, the area has been an isolated fortress in Amsterdam's center. Walled and guarded, the area has been unaffected by the surrounding development or any urban planning, and it has become, in fact, increasingly disconnected from the city as a whole. The recent economic crisis and the modernization of the Dutch military have motivated the owner, the Dutch national government, to consider alternative uses for the area and the transfer

The navy yard is an enclave that sits amid quickly changing surroundings of ownership. Its current, mostly military uses will either be relocated or become obsolete, thus creating new possibilities for the area to become an urban destination that is open to the general public.

The fact that, after some 260 years, the navy yard's approximately thirty acres will become available to new uses has greatly inspired Amsterdam's residents and others in Holland. Politicians, investors, developers, architects, tourist agencies, movie producers, and citizens alike all have ideas for new uses. The challenge is to use the positive momentum and energy as input for programming the site. At the same time, in order to avoid giving into initial deals that might jeopardize the best use of this strategic location in the long term, the state, as an owner, sought collaboration with the city. The government has agreed to an approach of gradual transformation, using an organic growth model as a basis for a powerful mix of functions and activities. An agreed-upon, broad strategic plan defines the key criteria with which any future development plan must comply. On the one hand, these criteria consist of financial targets; on the other hand, they also comprise intangible values, such as the preservation of the site's important historic and cultural meaning to Dutch society.

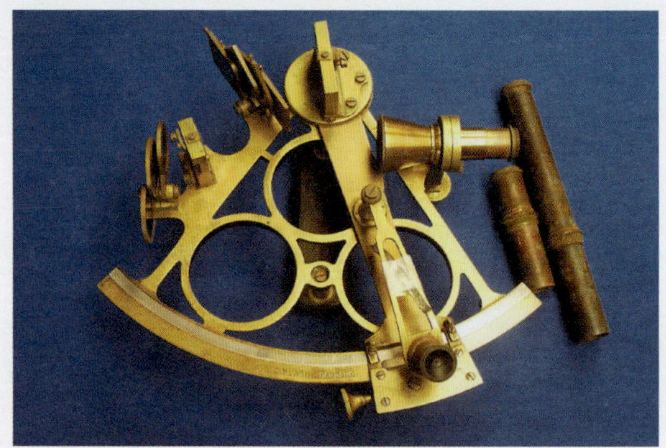

Technological innovation enabled the discovery of new territories

A ca. 1660 engraving by Ludolph Backhuyzen showing the naval shipyard with the current Nautical Museum in background

The intent to jointly develop the navy yard was formalized in a cooperation agreement between the City of Amsterdam and the national government in December 2013, just at the time when the Bass studio's work was being exhibited at ARCAM. Fortunately, early on, it was decided not to maximize short-term value by selling the site to the highest bidder. The Department of Defense will gradually evacuate the site through 2018, when all of it, including the existing buildings, will be available for new functions or dismantling. In the meantime, temporary activities will take place on the site, contributing to the development strategy. This temporary, agile development approach will, ultimately, fully integrate the site with Amsterdam by 2030.

The state and city have agreed on a number of themes that form the frame of reference for the selection of future users and development plans. The most important themes are maritime history, innovation, and, in the broadest sense of the word, water. The intent is not so much to use iconic architecture to increase the visibility of the site as part of the urban fabric but to identify users and functions that have a link with the above themes.

Initial Steps

The state and city have provided a start-up budget for the gradual transformation of the site. These funds will allow for the management of the process of finding actual renters, refurbishing the terrain's infrastructure, programming events, and research. Ahead of any lengthy planning processes, the transformation already is occurring and has had various positive spin-offs. The visibility of the site is being enhanced through a variety of new tenants who use the improved facilities temporarily for events and have increased accessibility by exposing the site to the general public, putting it on the public's mental map. This gradual approach allows for the development of a well-considered scheme.

Early in 2014, Liesbeth Jansen was asked to form and lead Bureau Navy Yard Amsterdam, a small organization that is managing the initial transformation process. The approach is explained below.

Getting the Feel

The first task was to research the site and its surroundings. An interdisciplinary project team mapped the site's history, demographics, city planning, economic infrastructure, environmental vulnerabilities, architectural typologies, and, perhaps most important, the diversity and mix of the current residents.

Photographs of Marine Etablissement Personnel and writers from The Land Inside Walls exhibition

Known for its adventures on the high seas, exploration of new territories, and celebration of new techniques and technologies, the city's character is preceded by centuries of history. This mix of courage, discipline, and persistence is also inscribed on the site: for the past hundred years, it has acted as a navy base, a fortress protecting the city.

The linkage between the neighborhood and the base proved to be a source of intriguing stories and secrets. To help the general public gain an understanding of the significance, history, and use of the venue, a number of artists collected stories and images that, taken together, form an overarching narrative—orally, textually, and visually. Photographer Koos Breukel made portraits of navy personnel and writers in a series of photographs that was exhibited on site and published in the book *Het land binnen de muren* (*The Land Inside Walls*), which was enthusiastically received by both navy personnel and their non-commissioned neighbors.

Pioneering Spirit

In January 2015, the so-called Front Yard was made available for public use. It includes a small, park-like area with its own access gate, one historic building, and a few buildings from the 1960s. Within four months, all the available space was leased to tech, film, innovation, television, and educational organizations and companies that exhibited Amsterdam's pioneering spirit: Werkplaats Archeologie BMA, Crosswise Works, Open State Foundation, Micanti, TV Academy, The App Academy, Orientation Travel Production, Sandberg Instituut/Designing Democracy, StartupDelta, Drain Products, Studio Zeitgeist, Glimworm, Amsterdam Smart City, and Pension Homeland, among others. One of the key goals in the early stages was to select partners/tenants that not only match the above-described themes and values but also have a pioneering spirit and are willing to share knowledge and networks. The notion that, today, many of these tenants might not be financially solvent has been proven wrong: they all pay market rents.

Basic Upgrading

After the partial conveyance of the site, the Bureau Navy Yard Amsterdam took over its maintenance, which included the seawalls, and made insertions of hard and soft infrastructure, such as digital cables, security, and facility management. Preparations for the construction of a temporary bridge to improve the connection with the Central Station are in an advanced state. A 2,500 square-meter vacant building is being renovated to accommodate a variety of new functions, and one of the existing tenants is modifying another building to become a "guest house for professionals," called Pension Homeland. The bureau has also started to organize presentations and events in the chief of naval staff's former residence. These activities enhance the site's visibility and are begining to generate substantial revenues.

At this stage, all physical interventions are temporary and revocable. So, no new buildings will be built, and renovations ensure flexibility in future use. Most renovations are financed by the tenants.

Public participation is highly encouraged in workshops on subjects such as "the history of the yard," "sports," and "circular economy." Because the yard is not yet part of the public realm, the usual public planning procedures do not yet apply. Public participation offers an alternative and effective way to interact with neighbors and other interested citizens.

Neighbors visit the future Pension Homeland

JLG LIFT

A navy-yard building with three stories of multifunctional space renovated in 2016 by Architects Bureau SLA, Amsterdam

Connecting

From a research map of downtown Amsterdam building functions, it became clear that the navy yard is a monolithic island in a very diverse city, a disposition that will gradually change. For example, the number of physical connections—bridges, roads, entrance gates—will increase between the site and the city. Furthermore, collaborations in programming on topics such as maritime history, energy innovation, and hydrology are sought with institutions in the immediate vicinity, including NEMO, the Kromhout Shipyard, ARCAM, the Eastern Church, the Amsterdam Central Library, and the van Gendt-halls. This may lead to a new thematic urban quarter, crossing the existing physical and legal boundaries.

Many neighborhood residents consider upcoming changes a potential threat. Development could have a major impact on their surroundings: Rents might increase to a level they cannot afford, traffic may intensify, and new demographic groups could move into the neighborhood. At the same time, local residents might have new employment opportunities and will be able to enjoy the navy yard's quiet, open space, which are rare commodities in downtown Amsterdam.

Planning

Many elements will influence the phasing of the site's development. For instance, it is still uncertain exactly when and how the navy will complete its evacuation and the state its conveyance of full ownership to the city. Moreover, access and site activities will be hampered during the first six months of 2016, when ministers, heads of state, and their entourage, will descend upon the capital (and site) for a series of conferences, as the Netherlands will be chairing the European Union. Temporary structures will be built, and security measures will be increased. Of course, these special events will enhance the site's visibility even further, but they could also cause deviations from its currently intended uses and the development time schedule.

A Method Exists in the Madness

Organic development does not mean to lean backward and wait to see what happens. Rather, it requires a very proactive approach and clearly defined goals. In this case, the purpose is to make the navy yard a valuable addition to the urban fabric of Amsterdam that is meaningful to its residents and other local and national economic and public stakeholders.

The Agile Transformation of a Navy Yard

The approach to the development of the navy yard requires flexibility, skill, and a certain lightheartedness—qualities that suit the rapid and often unpredictable changes in today's society. Setting short-term, tangible goals reduces the risk of failing to meet the community's current and future needs. As mirrored in the software industry's successes, the development of a site likewise demands project management that is commanding and agile but that also shares responsibility for the process and the results with other stakeholders.

Organic processes of urban development create maneuvering room for adaptation, experimentation, and improvisation so that the optimal, most suitable solutions for the development can be found. An occasional wrong choice is inevitable. However, to reduce the risk of derailment, small steps, in terms of duration and scale, are taken when choosing activities and functions. This approach creates room for easy corrective measures. In the case of the navy yard, this wiggle room also means that, in the short term, no irrevocable major development decisions will be taken. While this approach might be frustrating for certain investors, developers, and planners, it will ultimately lead to a better-functioning city than would bold, large-scale development steps.

In the long term, the values of the past, transposed and projected into the future, will create a strong and unique identity that is beyond bricks and mortar and provide the framework for resilient new uses for this unique site.

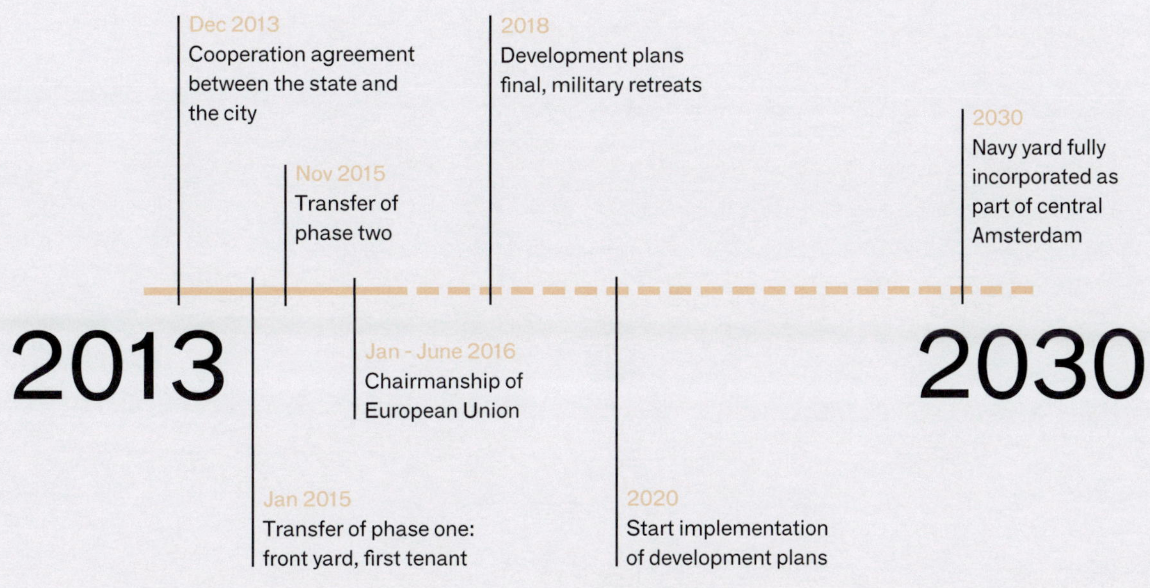

06

Site photography near the Marine Etablissement showing a pedestrian bridge and the NEMO science center as seen from the Oosterdokseiland

Isaäc
Kalisvaart

—Isaäc M. Kalisvaart

With great pleasure, I took on the task of being a Bass Fellow to broaden the students' awareness of the many issues that come into play when developing good urban places, which, as a developer, I consider to be my key mission. During the studio, the students were required to consider the history of the location, the urban context, mitigating strategies for risks involved in planning and construction, the interests of the multiple stakeholders, and the reality of the financial and real estate markets. Because of the limited time available, not all aspects could be considered sufficiently in most of the final development schemes. However, I believe that the studio, including the daily discussions and the (on occasion, emotional) jury reviews, has deepened the students' understanding of the wide-ranging issues that influence the development process, from the research and conceptual phase to completion. The studio has no doubt influenced the students' notion of the role and many responsibilities of the architect.

I must compliment the students for coming up with often innovative mixes of functions and typologies, that sparked the imagination of myself and others. The discussions that we organized in connection with the exhibition of the students' projects in the Architecture Centre of Amsterdam could have a permanent impact on the future development direction of the navy yard, giving the students' learning experience a pressing, real-time relevance.

For myself, my time at Yale has forced me, as a developer, to reflect on the essential lessons learned, which were important to pass on to these aspiring architects who will become responsible for shaping our future living environment. And to do that in an institution of academic excellence such as Yale was a great privilege.

Finally, I would like to thank Dean Robert Stern for appointing me, my fellow teachers of the studio—Alex Garvin, Kevin Gray, Erik Go, Andrei Harwell, and Hans-Hugo Smit—for their valuable contributions and friendship, the jury members for their insightful comments, and the students for inspiring us all.

View of a historic warehouse in the Czar Peterbuurt neighborhood of Amsterdam

WARNING !

A construction tour of MAB's OMA-designed De Rotterdam project

The Spuiplein in
Den Haag

Credits

Alexander Garvin

Alexander Garvin has combined a career in urban planning and real estate with teaching, architecture, and public service. He is currently president and CEO of AGA Public Realm Strategists, Inc., a planning and design firm in New York City that is responsible for the initial master plans for the Atlanta BeltLine, Tessera (a 700-acre [283-hectare] community outside Austin, Texas), and Hinton Park, in Collierville, Tennessee. Between 1996 and 2005, he was managing director for planning at NYC2012, the committee to bring the Summer Olympics to New York City in 2012. During 2002–03, he was vice president for planning, design, and development of the Lower Manhattan Development Corporation. Over the last forty-five years, he has held prominent positions in five New York City administrations, including deputy commissioner of housing and city planning commissioner.

Garvin is adjunct professor of urban planning and management at Yale University, where he has taught a wide range of subjects, including "Introduction to the Study of the City," for more than forty-nine years. In addition, he teaches three courses in the School of Architecture, including: "An Introduction to Planning & Real Estate Development," "Residential Design, Development, and Management," and "Intermediate Planning & Development."

Garvin is the author of *The American City: What Works, What Doesn't*; *The Planning Game: Lessons from Great Cities*; and *Public Parks: The Key to Livable Communities*. In 2016, Island Press will publish his next book, *What Makes a Great City*.

Kevin D. Gray

Kevin D. Gray, FRICS, received his M.Arch from the University of Pennsylvania and his MBA from the Yale School of Management. He is a principal at Kevin D Gray Consulting and has been responsible for more than $500 million in equity transactions and advised on over $2 billion in consulting and valuation assignments. Gray is a former managing director of real estate investment banking for PricewaterhouseCoopers Securities and the editor, with John R. White, of *Shopping Centers and Other Retail Properties.* He is also a licensed real estate appraiser and broker and a registered architect.

Gray is a Fellow of the Royal Institute of Chartered Surveyors and a member of the International Council of Shopping Centers. Gray is lecturer

Touring recently-completed multi-family housing in Het Funenpark, a re-developed area east of the Marine Etablissement site

in the practice of real estate at both the Yale School of Management and the Yale School of Architecture, where he teaches courses on real estate finance and investment and the history of real estate ownership.

Erik Go

Erik Go is a real estate concept developer and designer. Working with developers, investors, cities, and architects, he creates new strategies and concepts that add long-term value to buildings and neighborhoods.

Go's interest and expertise in mixed-use real estate and the way it shapes today's cities is a common theme throughout his career. His portfolio includes award-winning retail, leisure, health, office, and residential projects, such as De Rotterdam, Palais Quartier Frankfurt, Clichy Batignolles Paris, Achter de Lange Stallen Breda, ABC Shopping Achrafieh Beirut, Harvey Nichols Manchester, and many more.

As head of design at MAB Development, he co-organized and lectured in the studio at Yale. Go holds degrees in architecture (Delft) and architectural research (London) and received training in shopping-center development, design management, and design thinking.

Go lives in the Netherlands and currently works with his company ONE.GO on real estate concepts throughout Europe.

Liesbeth Jansen and Maarten Pedroli

Liesbeth Jansen is project director for Bureau Navy Yard Amsterdam and also director of Linkeroever "Left Bank," where she works as an independent consultant in the area of redevelopment and creative entrepeneurship. Jansen, together with Maarten Pedroli, focuses her work on the re-activation of buildings and vacant areas.

Linkeroever enables (re-)development through feasibility analysis, (re-)positioning, communication, programming, and financial analysis. The firm is currently involved in numerous transformation projects. Previously, Jansen was with MAB Development, a principal force in the redevelopment of the Westergasfabriek, in Amsterdam.

Isaäc Kalisvaart

Isaäc Kalisvaart has been an international real estate developer for most of his professional career, both as an entrepreneur and corporate executive. He obtained his master's degree in civil engineering at Delft University of Technology and an MBA degree at INSEAD, in Fontainebleau, France. After working for several years as a civil engineer in the Middle East, he moved to the U.S. and developed mostly resort and residential properties in the Caribbean and the Pacific Northwest. Subsequently, he became CEO of MAB Development, a leader in large urban transformations in Europe, and developed many large, urban mixed-use schemes in major cities in Western Europe. Project examples are Oosterdokseiland in Amsterdam, a €700 million mixed-use transformation of a former postal distribution facility, next to Central Station in Amsterdam, and Palais Quartier, in Frankfurt, a €1 billion plus urban mixed-use project in downtown Frankfurt. He has worked with many renowned architects, most recently with Rem Koolhaas on De Rotterdam, a 150,000 square-meter (1.6 million square-foot), mixed-use building in Rotterdam. Kalisvaart is professionally inspired by deal-making, the physical transformation of the public domain, and architecture. He recently resigned from his company and is currently advising the boards of several companies. He also participates in various start-ups. Kalisvaart loves the visual arts and has been on the board of several cultural institutions (Bouwfonds Art Foundation, Sculpture Museum "Beelden aan Zee," Rembrandthuis).

Hans-Hugo Smit

Hans-Hugo Smit is an urban geographer and city developer. His professional career is focused on understanding how people use space and how the built environment can better meet human needs. Believing in the power of cities, Smit is a contributor to sustainable and meaningful urban places where people live, work, shop, and simply be.

As a researcher, concept developer, and academic lecturer—with fifteen years of experience in the field of housing and retail real estate—Smit focuses on client-oriented urban development and contributes to the design, development, and marketing of living environments that are based on a thorough knowledge of customer and stakeholder needs. Working as a market analyst at MAB Development, he co-organized and taught the 2013 Bass development studio at the Yale School of Architecture. Smit holds degrees in human geography and city development. He currently lives in Amsterdam, working as concept developer at BPD Development, one of Europe's leading urban development companies.

Lunch at a café in MAB's Westergasfabreik project in Amsterdam

Studio Instructors:

Isaäc Kalisvaart, Alexander Garvin, Kevin D. Gray, Andrei Harwell, Erik Go, and Hans-Hugo Smit.

Yale M.Arch Students:

Jonas Barre, Todd Christensen, Owen Howlett, Jaeyoon Kim, Hochung Kim, Miron Nawratil, Matthew Rauch, Mathew Suen, and Jay Tsai.

Thanks also to the following architects, planning professionals and design critics who gave their time to assist the studio:

Ton Schaap, Paul Moons, Fritz van Dongen, Liesbeth Jansen, Carolien Schippers , Merijn Snoek, Maarten Kloos, Paul Kroese, James von Klemperer, Todd Reisz, Adib Cure, Elizabeth Plater-Zyberk, and Lucy Wildrick.

Receptie

A walk through the atrium of Den Haag's City Hall, a building by Richard Meier and Partners

Image Credits

Alexander Garvin: 52, 53, 57, 132, 172; Andrei Harwell: 153; Arjen Veldt and Architects Bureau SLA Amsterdam: 154; British Library Labs Project: 44, 45, 150; Erik Go: 164; Koos Bruekel : 152; MAB Development: 26, 28–30, 32–39; Mathew Suen: 6, 12, 17, 20, 42, 58, 120, 126, 160, 169; Matthew Rauch: 50, 51, 54, 139, 162, 174; Siebe Swart: 148, 149.